MANNERS

GOOD MANNERS ARE NEVER PASSÉ.

—Slim Aarons

395

SIMON & SCHUSTER
NEW YORK LONDON TORONTO SYDNEY

always gracious,
sometimes irreverent

MANNERS

BY

edited by Ruth Peltason and Julia Leach

illustrations by Virginia Johnson

For your birthday your sister gave you a bright yellow coat.
You adore her and would never want to hurt her feelings, but the yellow
makes your skin look sallow and the coat is a bit snug. Can you re-gift?

Re-gifting is one of the most delicate etiquette topics. If
your sister will notice the coat's disappearance, then
hang it in your closet. If your sister lives 2,000 miles away,
consider giving the coat to a friend. First and foremost,
keep in mind the feelings of the original gift-giver.

You're taking the red-eye from LA to New York, and the young man
sitting next to you has brought his own midnight snack. Orange peels
and half of a bologna sandwich remain on his tray well into
the in-flight movie. Do you have to grin and bear it?

There is more than one use for the air sickness bag.
With a warm smile, gently gesture toward the tray and volunteer
to scoop up the orange peels. This direct, yet kind hint should catch
his attention and prompt quick disposal of the offending items.

You're treating business clients to their favorite lunch at the
Grand Central Oyster Bar. One person lifts the shell and slurps
the oyster right into his mouth. Should you follow suit?

Apparently, your colleague last enjoyed oysters
at a beachfront bar. Unless you're in a casual place,
oysters should be eaten with a shellfish fork.
And never, ever attempt to cut these delicate treats.

HAVE YOU EVER WONDERED . . . ?

Spending a weekend at a friend's country house can be completely relaxing. Often, however, one experiences mild pangs of angst. Your friend and her husband are sleeping in, yet you've been up since 7 AM and are craving a cup of coffee. Is it okay to brew a pot?

 Consider your relationship with your hosts. If you've been coming to their home for years, then by all means make some coffee, but take care not to wake them. If you're visiting new friends, don't overstep your bounds in their home; instead, distract yourself with the morning paper.

You're hosting a festive dinner party and learn the afternoon of the gathering that your brother will be bringing his new girlfriend. She's wonderful, charming, and she's a vegan. How can you quickly prepare to meet her culinary needs?

Presumably at this late hour, the shrimp is marinating, and it's likely that salad, which should be appealing to your brother's girlfriend, is already on the menu. During cocktails, set out some fresh fruit; when dinner is ready, refresh the fruit plate and keep it on the table. Most importantly, make your vegan guest feel at ease and avoid referring to her dietary preferences.

For the past few months you have been working on a big project and have over-looked some personal matters, large and small. One of them is a letter you intended to send to your aunt, thanking her for the floral shirt she gave you at Christmas. Now that it's April, is it too late to send a note?

It's never too late to send a thank-you note. Your aunt, who may be disappointed by your lack of communication, will be glad to hear from you and know that all is well. In the future, keep a box of thank-you's handy (pre-stamped if your schedule is that frantic) and remember that the ten minutes it takes to express your thanks will be time well spent.

HAVE YOU EVER WONDERED...?

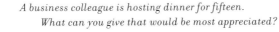

A business colleague is hosting dinner for fifteen.
What can you give that would be most appreciated?

Although wine is a customary hostess gift, it's likely that she's already selected a red and a white. Since flowers are always a crowd pleaser, this is a safe token. Arriving with them is always thoughtful; better still, send the flowers early the day of the gathering.

Traveling to Japan for the first time on business, you receive an invitation to a formal
tea ceremony. What can you expect and how should you behave?

Simply prepare to eat, drink, and be (quietly) merry. The host has spent a great deal of time preparing the food, flowers, and scrolls, and as a guest your most important responsibility is to compliment her or him on each of these elements. Be sure to write a thank-you note within three days of the ceremony. This is known as *korei,* "thanking afterwards."

You're at your in-laws for Thanksgiving dinner and have been asked to set the table.
They have twice as many forks than you usually use, as well as extra spoons.
What are the basics of setting formal flatware?

If the plates will be on the table when guests are seated, place the napkin to the left of (not under) the first-course, main-course, and salad forks. Knives, with blades facing the plate, and the soupspoon are placed to the right of the plate. The dessert fork and spoon are placed above the plate, the spoon on top facing left, and the fork underneath with tines facing right.

You're a bridesmaid in your brother's summer wedding in Nantucket. His fiancée has chosen dresses that are vaguely nautical, but your personal style is Comme des Garçons. Are you obliged to wear the dress during the reception?

With any luck, your brother will get married only once. So while boating insignia may not reflect your personal taste, in the spirit of the event wear the dress with a smile. Unless they've encouraged everyone in the party to change clothes, stay the course, enjoy the evening, and toast to the lovely couple's future.

At the end of a long evening, you're helping a close friend straighten up. While neatening the couch, you knock a vase off the console and it crashes to the floor. You know she brought it home from her honeymoon in Greece. What to do?

Some situations are inherently unpleasant, and this is one of them. It's incumbent on you to offer a sincere apology and understand that the broken vase may cause your friend considerable dismay. If the break was clean, gently insist on arranging to have a specialist handle the repair. If the vase shattered, don't get overly emotional—leave that to your friend. In either case, the next day follow up with a note of apology and a small bouquet.

You and a friend are enjoying happy hour when the bartender sets down a tequila sunrise from the man across the bar. Do you accept? Show interest? Whose move is it?

Protocol suggests that the ball is in your court. While you're not obligated to accept the cocktail, rejecting it sends a firm message. If you're interested in moving beyond significant eye contact, a subtle smile and lingering gaze should get him up off his barstool.

CONTENTS

THE WORLD IS ROUND, AND MANNERS AREN'T SQUARE

"Etiquette means behaving yourself a little better than is absolutely necessary."

—Will Cuppy

Yankee pride, Southern charm, California laissez-faire, Texan hospitality, and Midwestern manners—all are phrases we use to communicate a certain welcoming quality and friendly state-of-mind. When I meet people and tell them I'm from Kansas City, they assume I'm going to behave well and with kindness. It's a Midwestern "thing," they say, that down-home quality bred in the American heartland. In my opinion, as far as manners go, the true American heartland extends from coast to coast and points in between. Much of my work involves travel, and I have been fortunate to meet nice people all over the country.

So why a book about manners? And are we just preaching to the choir? My husband, Andy, and I believe that good manners are the essence of communication. For years we've had a tradition in our office that each new employee is welcomed with a copy of Emily Post's etiquette book. Consider Mrs. Post's words, wise when first written eighty years ago, and still meaningful today: "Charm cannot exist without good manners—meaning by this, not so much manners that precisely follow particular rules, as manners that have been made smooth and polished by the continuous practice of kind impulses." What a perfect definition of a caring and cultured society!

I've been inspired by Emily Post for years, as well as by many people in my own life who have in their unique way demonstrated the bounty that good etiquette brings. Now, in *Manners*, I've tried to cover topics that seem part of the way we live today—the overnight guest, cell phone behavior, even the etiquette of bicycling on city streets. Americans have long had a love affair with food and with dining out, and to that end I have included some of my observations on table manners, including those for children. (On the subject of manners at the table, I would like to add that you may feed your dog table scraps *as long as no guests are present*. That seems fair to me. And to my dog, Henry.) You'll find recommendations on tipping, both during the year and at holidays, and suggestions for being a good traveler, whether at home or abroad. For those of you who are globe-trotters, the international welcome mat should be respected. The key is learning the rules of being a goodwill ambassador wherever you go.

Of course, life isn't perfect—someone calls you by the wrong name, your wine spills, an invitation never arrives, or you're an hour early for cocktails or a week late for an appointment. It happens, and for every social disaster, gracious recovery is available. There are examples of things we've all experienced, which I hope will help you grapple with the occasional social stumbling block. But for all the specific advice in the world, I can say that nothing beats humor and graciousness as antidotes to nearly any social faux pas. The last section of *Manners* touches upon a miscellany of topics—lending books, double dipping, borrowing clothes from a friend, the night-owl neighbor, re-gifting, and money (an endless source of consternation).

My hope is that *Manners* helps to ensure what Emily Post called "the continuous practice of kind impulses." Life is a bowl of cherries—as long as you know what to do with the pits.

Kate Spade
New York City, 2003

THE DAILY LIFE OF MANNERS

MODERN-DAY ETIQUETTE

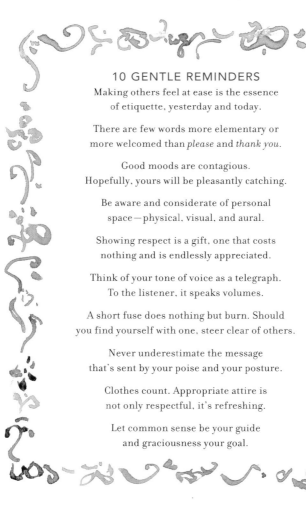

10 GENTLE REMINDERS

Making others feel at ease is the essence
of etiquette, yesterday and today.

There are few words more elementary or
more welcomed than *please* and *thank you*.

Good moods are contagious.
Hopefully, yours will be pleasantly catching.

Be aware and considerate of personal
space—physical, visual, and aural.

Showing respect is a gift, one that costs
nothing and is endlessly appreciated.

Think of your tone of voice as a telegraph.
To the listener, it speaks volumes.

A short fuse does nothing but burn. Should
you find yourself with one, steer clear of others.

Never underestimate the message
that's sent by your poise and your posture.

Clothes count. Appropriate attire is
not only respectful, it's refreshing.

Let common sense be your guide
and graciousness your goal.

AT HOME, YOURS OR OTHERS

Hospitality is first learned at home, where *good morning* and *good night* are first expressed, and where the common experiences of everyday life are discussed. Being a team player and showing consideration of others are essential around family and close friends. Once you learn the ABCs of good behavior at home, you'll also become everyone's favorite guest.

TABLE MANNERS

Which fork or how many glasses, and ways to navigate a forkful of peas are rudimentary lessons of being *à table* without calling attention to yourself. Table manners are a skill that once mastered last a lifetime, and will take you from the picnic table to White House receptions (should you be invited).

THE 9-TO-5

The planet called "your office" is where you spend more time each week than anywhere else (except perhaps in your bed, sleeping). Doing your work well and being collegial are assets that will stay with you throughout your career, and in whatever field you pursue.

MANNERS ON THE MOVE

Plains, trains, and automobiles may take you from Point A to Point B, but bear in mind that you're often in the company of hundreds of strangers. The more you both "speak the same language," the smoother the ride.

DRESS ETIQUETTE

Nothing's wrong with your shirt tail out — if you're gardening. Showing an appreciation for time and place are reflected first in your appearance; it's often what leaves a lasting impression, as well. Personal grooming and style are your calling card wherever you go.

IN THE PUBLIC EYE

Do you hold the door for someone older? How generous should you be with holiday tips? These are questions often raised when considering manners at large. Of course popcorn and movies are ideal mates, but not everyone agrees, so best to chew quietly.

AT HOME, YOURS OR OTHERS

"If you were at my house, your comfort would matter most to me. So I'd try to think of ways to make you feel at ease, or do my best to anticipate what you might want."

BEFORE YOUR GUESTS ARRIVE...

A welcoming household takes work, and behind-the-scenes preparations will make your company feel relaxed.

Sweep the front walk and turn on the lights. Nothing suggests an inviting home more than the friendly glow from lights seen upon arriving.

Fluff the couch pillows, but don't overly "style" them—after all, your guest is in your home, not in a hotel lobby.

Have snacks prepared, as well as white and red wine, soda, and juice.

If it's wintertime, have logs on hand for a fire.

Set out fresh flowers. If house lights say "welcome," then flowers offer a warm smile.

A bathroom being shared with your company should be cleared of overly personal effects. Be sure to put out a fresh bar of soap and guest towels, and a scented candle.

If you have children, scoop up errant toys and games from public spaces.

And be ready before your company arrives. Nothing's more awkward for the guest than watching her host run around tidying up.

WHEN YOU WELCOMED YOUR GUESTS, THE SUN WAS SHINING...

Have umbrellas handy for any departing guests who would otherwise get soaked getting from your front door to their car or to a cab.

"Basically, I think the kitchen is off-limits to guests. However, if one of my close friends who loves to cook wants to help, then I'm thrilled."

IDEALS TO ASPIRE TO...

"The ideal guest is an equally ideal hostess; the principle of both is the same: a ready smile, a quick sympathy, a happy outlook, [and] consideration for others. . . ."

—Emily Post, *Etiquette*

WHEN YOU'RE THE GUEST...

Don't stand on ceremony, and don't sit on the arms of chairs and couches, either—Be natural but not overly familiar.

Be a team player—Whether your hosts suggest watching *King Kong*, playing Scrabble, or sitting on the porch (even though it's chilly), be eager and accommodating.

Exercise restraint—Feet belong on the floor, not on the furniture; don't assume a bowl of fresh raspberries has only your name on it; and if your host doesn't sleep in, then neither should you.

Be prepared—If your hosts are tennis players or they're having friends in for cocktails, then plan ahead and bring the proper clothes.

Want to be invited back?—If you've stayed for the weekend and didn't arrive with a hostess gift, be sure to send a note and a small gift, ideally no more than two weeks after your visit.

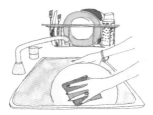

"I always prefer to take care of cleaning up after everyone has gone home—sometimes even the next day. As a guest, I find it distracting to hear the *clinkety-clink* of dishes coming from the kitchen. Besides, there's no faster way to kill a party atmosphere than to start rounding up glasses and so forth. The point is for you and your guests to relax and enjoy yourselves."

"IT WAS A DELIGHTFUL VISIT—PERFECT, IN BEING MUCH TOO SHORT."
—JANE AUSTEN, *EMMA*

TABLE MANNERS

"I don't think that table manners are passé. Since everyone is in plain sight of everyone else, it's pretty obvious if you slurp your soup or hoard the bread basket. Does anyone enjoy being at a table with a loud mouth or messy eater?"

The dining table is intended for china, glassware, utensils, and linens. Key chains, lipstick, the mail, and children's toys are best placed elsewhere at mealtime.

"AS THE SHIPS SAIL OUT TO SEA, I SPOON MY SOUP AWAY FROM ME."

"Higher emotions are what separate us from the lower orders of life . . . higher emotions, and table manners."

—Deanna Troi,
from *Star Trek: The Next Generation*

COLOR THAT LASTS

There's a practical explanation for the word *lipstick* —the color actually does *stick*, so before a meal don't overdo it and leave behind a trail of red on your dinner napkin. If you want to touch up your lipstick after a meal, it's best to excuse yourself from the table. (But lip balm, used discreetly, is permissible at the table.)

BODY LANGUAGE

You might need to lean on your elbows if you're dining out and are seated at a small table in a crowded restaurant. But at home, where the table is ample and ambient sound is comfortable, avoid placing your elbows on the table. (And never hunch over and "hug" your plate.)

FINGER BOWLS

"I love when little finger bowls are used, especially after eating ribs or shellfish. I find that gives me a chance to clean up without having to excuse myself from the table. And it also saves extra wear on the napkins."

AND DON'T FORGET...

When serving food, be sure that all your guests are taken care of before serving yourself.

Food should always be passed to the right, or counterclockwise.

If the dinner conversation is running long and you're inclined to yawn, either quietly excuse yourself or be clever and camouflage your fatigue.

When you are asked to pass the salt, pass the pepper, too.

NEXT TIME YOU'RE AT THE WHITE HOUSE

When dining with the president of the United States, a guest can respectfully assume that decorum and style are established by him, and, as such, are to be adopted. One evening President Coolidge invited some friends to dinner at the White House. When it came time for coffee, the president poured his into a saucer. So did his guests. Then Coolidge added some cream and sugar. His guests did the same. Then Coolidge leaned over and gave the saucer to the family cat.

"THE REAL TEST OF PERFECT TABLE MANNERS IS NEVER TO OFFEND THE SENSIBILITIES OF OTHERS."
—EMILY POST, *ETIQUETTE*

UTENSILS

THE LANGUAGE OF FLATWARE

Of all the traditional guidelines for handling a fork, knife, and spoon, two are especially useful. If you pause during the meal, set your fork on the left side of your plate, with the tines down, and the knife on the right, with the sharp edge facing in. When you're done, set your knife and fork beside one another on the right side of your plate, fork tines facing up or down.

YES, YOU CAN CUT YOUR SALAD...

If you find that your chopsticks are becoming more like pickup sticks in your hands, don't be shy: ask for a fork.

The lingering resistance dates back to the time when knife blades were made of silver, which interacted with the vinegar in the dressing. Today, since most flatware is stainless steel, cutting your salad is a matter of personal preference.

NAPKINS

After being seated, wait until your host has joined the table and lifted his or her napkin, then place yours neatly on your lap.

When excusing yourself from the table between courses, place your napkin on your seat or the arm of your chair. (And leave the table napkin-free.)

If you have an especially large or oversize napkin, first fold it in half and then place it on your lap.

BEFORE YOU LEAVE THE TABLE

When you're done with the meal, simply rest your napkin to the left of the place setting. If the plates have already been cleared, then place it neatly on the table in front of you, but not as originally folded.

PORTIONS

Unless you've just bicycled fifty miles and are ravenous, start with moderate portions. You can always take seconds when they're offered, but when you do be sure to compliment the cook.

Leaving food on your plate is not a sign of good manners. But eating what you've served yourself is.

Take small portions of everything. Overcooked, undercooked, burnt, and zealously spiced are not good reasons to pass up a dish—unless, of course, you're allergic!

DRINKS

WHEN SERVING WINE...

QUANTITY—For a dinner party, estimate one bottle of wine for every two people. Even if you wind up with extra, it's better than not having enough.

WINEGLASSES—Set out glasses for each type of wine you plan to serve.

THE SEQUENCE—White before red, and dry before sweet is traditional.

HOLD THE GLASS JUST SO...

For room-temperature wines, hold wineglasses or goblets under the bowl. Chilled wines (whites and rosés) should be held by the stem of the glass. As for champagne, choose the base or the stem, depending on your glassware.

"Mrs. Givings, sitting tense as a coiled snake on the edge of the sofa, gently closed her eyes and wanted to die. Sherry in a highball glass!"

—Richard Yates, *Revolutionary Road*

FINGER FOODS

Hors d'oeuvres are one of the few foods that adults are encouraged to eat with their fingers. That said, there are pitfalls to avoid. In addition to certain hors d'oeuvres, there are more common foods that require a bit of dexterous handling, such as the proverbial "hot dog with everything" at the ball game.

CHERRY TOMATOES—This is a one-bite food, so choose your tomato wisely.

BUFFALO CHICKEN WINGS AND SPARERIBS—It's assumed that spicy wings and ribs are finger food, so enjoy yourself. But be sure to have a "bone bucket" on hand before digging in.

PIZZA—Even the common "slice" can be eaten with grace. Hold the pizza with your fingers and curl the sides so that the topping doesn't slide.

RADISHES AND CELERY—If garnishes are passed at dinner, spoon them onto your butter or cocktail plate. If the radishes aren't neatly trimmed and the celery still has its "feathers," make as discreet and tidy a pile as possible on the side of your plate.

SHRIMP—One dip and two bites are recommended. The tail should be disposed of as quickly as is convenient.

CORN ON THE COB—Whether you eat yours typewriter style (across) or around, the cleanest way to eat fresh corn is to salt and butter it as you go. On the other hand, if you're among close friends or family, you may not need to be as tidy—so long as you don't let familiarity breed poor manners.

DEVILED EGGS—This always delicious food is also always messy. No one expects you to eat this in one bite (unless you want beaver cheeks), so use a napkin and be as tidy as possible.

CAVIAR—Use the serving spoon to put some caviar on your plate, and your own knife or spoon to gently prepare your portion. Take care not to overload your cracker or toast point with the sieved chopped egg and caviar. Nothing is worse (and more wasteful) than little grains of expensive caviar falling onto the carpet.

ASPARAGUS—Although not traditionally considered a finger food, there are times when you can pick up the asparagus and eat a single stalk. It's easier to plate this vegetable and use a knife and fork.

FRENCH FRIES—No fork ever made French fries taste better. Use your fingers and enjoy yourself.

TROUBLE FOODS

Some foods can be described as "trouble foods" because they pose a problem: what do you do with leftover shells and bones? What's a discreet way to bite into a triple-decker club sandwich? And what about fruit pits and banana peels? Nothing is more awkward than trying to take a spoonful of French onion soup au gratin and winding up with a skein of cheese a foot long. (If it happens, twirl the cheese around your soupspoon.)

FRUITS, JUICY AND OTHERWISE—Fruits that are juicy are best peeled and eaten with a knife and fork. So-called dry fruits, such as apples and pears, may be sliced and eaten with your fingers. Peeling is optional.

DISTASTEFUL FOOD—Have courage and camouflage your displeasure. Have a sip of water or wine to help mitigate the problem.

OVERSIZE SANDWICHES—This is not a contest between you and the sandwich. Triple-deckers or megasize roast beef sandwiches are best cut into smaller, more manageable pieces. Always use a knife and fork to eat an open-faced sandwich.

PEAS—These are always a challenge for the Artful Eater. You might need a pusher, such as a piece of bread or your knife, to help get the peas onto your fork. The alternatives: gently spear the peas with your fork tines or abstain.

ICE CREAM CONE AT THE BEACH—Even though children beg for it, sand and sun are the natural enemies of ice cream. It's not such a good idea, unless you're a very speedy eater or sitting on the boardwalk.

FRUIT AND OLIVE PITS

These do not go into your napkin, but are best placed in the cup of your hand and set on the side of your plate. This applies to watermelon seeds, too.

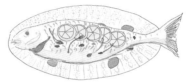

FISH BONES

Never, ever swallow. Instead, remove the bones from your mouth as discreetly as possible and place them on the side of your plate.

DARE I EAT A PEACH?

"If you are able to eat a peach in your fingers and not smear your face, let juice run down, or make a sucking noise, you are the one in a thousand who *may*, and with utmost propriety, continue the feat."

—Emily Post, *Etiquette*

EMBARRASSMENT MANEUVERS

Your soup dribbles down your shirtfront, you accidentally squirt your seatmate when you squeeze lemon on your salmon, or the table leg you kicked turns out to be the person directly across from you. These are among the hazards that can befall even the most conscientious diner. Fortunately, for every accident there truly is a remedy.

NAVIGATING TROUBLE AT THE TABLE...

HOT FOOD AND BEVERAGES—If you've taken a sip of your coffee or soup and it's too hot, quickly swallow some water. The same holds true for very hot food. Whatever you do, don't spit it out.

"WAITER, THERE'S A FLY IN MY SOUP!"

"KEEP IT DOWN, SIR, OR
THEY'LL ALL BE WANTING ONE."

THE UNEXPECTED "GARNISH"—Insects and food may be part of nature, but they don't belong together in a dish, whether at home or in a restaurant. If you're at someone's home, quietly tell your hostess about the problem; she should remove the offending dish with the utmost discretion. (Take care not to embarrass or offend anyone.) If you're at a restaurant, discretion is still called for, and yes, you're within your rights to expect an apology.

TOOTHSOME TIDBITS—Despite the best intentions, little particles of food will nest in between your teeth, especially poppy and sesame seeds, salads, and corn. Their removal requires diplomacy and tact; whether a friend tells you or you become aware of the problem yourself, excuse yourself briefly from the table. Take care of the problem in private and away from others.

GESUNDHEIT!—First you feel a little itch in your nose, and then before you can reach for a handkerchief or tissue, you sneeze. It's the most human of incidents, but when it happens at the table be sure to turn your head away from the food and the guests. After the fact, a tissue (or your napkin) is nonetheless a reassuring gesture, but when you blow, don't honk!

"SPINACH BETWEEN YOUR TEETH IS
NOT CONSIDERED AN ACCESSORY."

BABIES, CHILDREN, AND TEENAGERS AT THE TABLE

Unless your company is your family, babies are best fed separately from the adults. Most young children find a roomful of adults about as much fun as heat rash, so unless you wish to see your children squirm and fidget, excuse them from dining with grown-ups. But teenagers toe the line between childhood and adulthood, and as such are ripe subjects for table manners.

A FEW WORDS OF ADVICE...

SEATING—To thwart an outbreak of giggles or other shenanigans, avoid clustering children together, especially siblings.

PICK YOUR BATTLES—For teenagers, pulling in their chairs, remembering their napkins, and taking reasonable portions is multi-tasking of the highest order. Be grateful for efforts large and small.

BE TOLERANT—Accept that children and adults at the table operate with different sets of standards. This includes laughter, too. After all, you're a parent, not a policeman, and you're both there to enjoy yourselves.

Tiffany's Table Manners for Teenagers dispenses sound advice with insouciant wit and charm . . .

"You don't have to wait for your hostess to start eating, but don't leap at your food like an Irish wolfhound."

"Don't put too much in your mouth at once. It looks as if you were brought up in a kennel."

"Remember that a dinner party is not a funeral that your hostess has invited you to because she thinks you are in dire need of food. You're there to be entertaining. Be gay. Do your part. Don't be a gloom."

THE GOOPS

The Goops they lick their fingers,
And the Goops they lick their knives;
They spill their broth on the tablecloth—
Oh, they lead disgusting lives!
The Goops they talk while eating,
And loud and fast they chew;
And that is why I'm glad that I
Am not a Goop—are you?

— Gelett Burgess

MY IDEA OF THE 9-TO-5

"We like to think of ourselves as having a modern office, and we believe it makes perfect sense to give each new employee a copy of Emily Post's etiquette book. To me, Emily Post is generous and cheerful. Much of her advice is good common sense, and I like that she has such a positive outlook and a dry sense of humor."

kansas city   new york   paris

TIMELINES

Repeated tardy arrivals, early departures, or excessive doctor's appointments during the workday actually do affect your coworkers. The clock on the wall is there to help you pace the day, not skip out on it.

PERFUME AT WORK

If there's one thing people can disagree about, it's perfume and cologne. If you want to wear a scent, take a modest approach and choose something with subtle notes. Strong or cheap perfumes may cause offense and are inappropriate.

Perhaps no office equipment is more abused than the telephone. All the more reason to bear in mind a few caveats when placing or receiving calls: your tone should be professional but friendly; be concise and straightforward; return calls and voice mail messages within a day; and reserve the speakerphone for only the most appropriate occasions.

ODOR-AMA

You've been putting in long hours, you're trying to finish a presentation, and you can't find time for a proper lunch hour. So you order in a hamburger. Or a pizza with pepperoni. Or Kung Pao Chicken. Result? Your colleagues feel the need to fumigate their offices and yours. A little self-policing and abstinence will not only keep the air fresher, but your office relationships won't suffer. Even Busy People need to be considerate.

BEING A GOOD CITIZEN

A good test of citizenship comes into play when you work in an office. Be responsible and replace the used coffee filter, invite a new colleague to lunch, or volunteer to help organize the office holiday party. Be fair. Be nice. Be loyal.

THE MANICURIST WILL (NOT) SEE YOU NOW

Whether you have a closed office or a cubicle, there is nothing professional about doing your nails at your desk. If you think you must, then you need to plan your time more carefully.

After all the care you put into the clothes you wear to the office, don't forget that your office needs to look presentable too.

ROMANCE IN THE OFFICE

If only more people heard this phrase and thought "oxymoron!," because so many of these sparks smolder, sputter, and leave singed feelings. The office romance that ends in marriage is rare. Be smart: do work in the office and romance on your own time.

IN A MANNER OF SPEAKING...NOSY PARKER

A busybody or snoop. Opinion varies as to the origin of the phrase, but the most applicable refers to English parkskeepers ("parkers") who liked to keep tabs on amorous dalliances in Hyde Park. "Funny thing about Callie: every time you saw her at the water cooler, she was deep in an Important Conversation with another colleague. No surprise she was nicknamed the nosy parker in the office."

IN THE PUBLIC EYE

"First impressions, and how you handle being out in public, are serious considerations for everyone. I'm reluctant to impose myself, so to me making a discrete entrance is a pretty safe approach. And it never hurts to have a warm smile ready. I think it makes other people feel relaxed."

For quick purchases and transactions, have your money or credit card ready. Both the cashier and the people behind you will appreciate this. (Avoid searching for loose change in the bottom of your purse, too.)

PEDESTRIAN YEAS AND NAYS

Walking on a sidewalk should be a harmless activity, but unless you live in a small town, you know that potential hazards await you on any city street.

THE PASSING LANE—Walk to the right, pass on the left. Adjust your pace and don't "tailgate" the person in front of you, either. Obey traffic lights and signs. As for jaywalking, it just isn't safe.

SIDEWALK ROLLERBLADERS AND CYCLISTS—No ambiguity here: wheels and city sidewalks are not meant to mix. Only baby strollers allowed.

SAUNTERERS AND SHOPPERS—The wild card of pedestrians. They stop and start unexpectedly; they switch "lanes" absentmindedly; and they're rarely in sync with the normal flow. The remedy: pass them. If you're the slow walker, enjoy your stroll, but be aware of the surrounding pace.

YOUR UMBRELLA, WET OR DRY—When passing someone tall, lower your umbrella to avoid grazing their eye; conversely, raise your umbrella over anyone shorter than you. Accept that some negotiation of sidewalk space will be necessary and adjust your umbrella accordingly. Once it stops raining, carry your umbrella on a vertical slant, tip facing down.

SIDEWALK GRATES—Only hazardous if you're wearing high heels!

WHAT FLOOR, PLEASE?
WHEN IN THE ELEVATOR...
Turn off portable CD players.

Remove your hat.

Passengers should allow those entering unblocked access.
For those entering, step in and to the side or back.

When your floor is approaching,
try to be close to the doors for exiting.

ROUND AND ROUND SHE GOES...
Whereas a man commonly opens a door for a woman to enter
first, the situation is reversed with a revolving door. In this case,
the man goes first and pushes the door for the woman, or else
he pushes it forward from the side and allows her to enter first.

ESCALATORS
The English win hands down when it comes to escalator etiquette:
keep to the right and leave the left side free for passing. Short
of that, do your best not to block or impede others, and if you're
the one doing the passing, remember to say "excuse me."

IT'S A GROCERY CART, NOT A GO-CART
There are a few tales of people meeting in the aisle of a grocery
store and falling in love, but most people who "bump" into
others in the aisles come closer to fisticuffs than romance.

AISLE ETIQUETTE—When you park your cart, hug the wall, not the center of the aisle;
before you turn a corner, look ahead to see if the lane is clear.

AT THE DELI COUNTER—Wherever there is a line of people waiting to be served, assume there
is a ticket machine and wait your turn; you can reasonably expect others to do likewise.

CHECKOUT LINE—The tension of waiting on line to pay up is worse than horses straining to
break at the gate: for some reason, at this point all people want is *out*. Patience truly is a virtue
in this case. If there is an express lane for ten items or fewer, do the math the old-fashioned
way—each item counts.

RANDOM ACTS OF KINDNESS—If the person behind you only has only one or two items
and you have several, be gracious and let him or her go first.

TIPPING

Not only is tipping a customary way of showing your appreciation for services, often the people you're tipping are those most in need of extra money. One school of thought is that you should tip regardless of the quality of the service; others feel that a tip is a direct reflection of good service, and thus is earned. Also consider the personal relationship you might have with someone, such as the waiter at your neighborhood diner. In the end, be generous yet fair.

FOOD AND DRINK

Restaurant check: 15% to 20%
Gratuity is usually included for groups of six or more.

Bartender: $1 per drink

Food delivery: 10% (in bad weather, 15%)

Hotel room service: 15% of the check

DAY OF BEAUTY

Hairdresser: 15% to 20%

Manicurist and pedicurist: 10% to 20%

Masseuse: 10% to 20%

MISCELLANY

Coat check: $1 to $2 per item

Ladies' room attendant: $1

Usher at the ball game (if shown to your seat): 50 cents to $1

Valet parking: $2 to $3

TRAVEL

Airport skycap: $1 or more per bag

Bellhop: $1 per bag

Taxi or hired car: 15% to 20%

HOLIDAY TIPPING

The gift of a holiday tip is a way of thanking certain people for taking care of you during the year. Depending on what you're able to spend and how many people are on your list, it's a good idea to plan ahead by putting money aside from time to time. It's also useful to keep track of who you tip and what you give each year.

APARTMENT BUILDING STAFF

In general, the cash you give is thanks for the help you've received during the year and is a reflection of the type of building and city you live in.

Doorman: $25 to $100

Superintendant: $30 to $100

Custodian: $20 to $30

Handyman: $10 to $30

HAIRDRESSER

The cost of a regular session (plus a small gift). Again, this depends on your relationship, the salon, and how frequently you have your hair cut.

BABYSITTER

The equivalent of two nights' pay (plus a small gift)

HEALTH CLUB

Locker room attendant: $5 to $10

Trainer: $50 (or more)

And don't forget the dry cleaner, housekeeper, dog groomer, lawn crew, and parking garage attendant.

RESTAURANTS

Among the pleasures of daily life is dining out. You don't have to cook or clean up, and you get to eat exactly what you want. The price you pay for this luxury isn't just for the food; it's for the relationship between you and the restaurant, and between you and your waiter.

RESPECT YOUR RESTAURANT

Arrive five to ten minutes
prior to your reservation.

Wait your turn to greet the hostess.

Dress in keeping with the
style and ambience of the restaurant.

Have the proper form of payment
("cash only" is usually non-negotiable).

DINING DILEMMAS—"LET'S HAVE DINNER"

Other than politics and sports teams, nothing has the potential to cause more angst among friends and couples than the question, "who pays?" If it's just you and a close friend, split the check or alternate paying for the whole tab. If one has invited the other, the expectation is that the invitee is being treated. (Some fair exceptions: a significant age difference requires senior to pay for junior; if it's a business meal, regardless of who issued the invite the bill is paid by the person who stands to gain more from the meal.)

"THER OUGHT T'BE SOME WAY T'EAT CELERY SO IT WOULDN'T SOUND LIKE YOU WUZ STEPPIN' ON A BASKET."

—KIN HUBBARD

The waitstaff (waiter, waitress, waitron) are trained to accommodate you—to a point. Be cordial and concise, and expect the same in kind. Service in a diner is different from service in a four-star restaurant, and you'll enjoy yourself more if you adjust your expectations accordingly.

MOVIES

Inexplicably, when the lights go down in a movie theater, bad behavior has a way of sneaking in. Forethought and sensitivity to those around you will help keep the experience enjoyable.

When you enter a row, face the people already seated.

Your coat belongs on your chair—not on one beside or in front of you.

Turn off cell phones and pagers.

If you must talk to your companion, do so infrequently and keep your voice very low.

Wait until the credits are rolling before standing up to leave.

POPCORN is one of the pleasures of moviegoing, but it can also be annoying to those around you. Chew but don't chomp, and be sure to take any leftover popcorn with you when the movie's over.

Candy with CRINKLY WRAPPERS and plastic bags should be opened before the movie begins, especially if it's a serious story.

Unhappy about someone else kicking your seat or CHATTING too loudly? Stay calm, be friendly, and address the problem as quietly as possible.

HEIGHT MATTERS

It seems so obvious, but it bears repeating: short people truly can't see over the heads of tall people. When you choose a seat, consider if the person behind you will be able to see. Be sure to remove your hat, whether it's a wide brim or a baseball cap.

"THE PEOPLE IN THE MOVIE SHOULD DO THE TALKING, NOT THE PEOPLE IN THE AUDIENCE."

MANNERS ON THE MOVE
IN A CAR, ON A TRAIN, PLANE, OR SUBWAY

As long as you observe some basic guidelines, traveling with hundreds of strangers on open highways or in close quarters can bring unexpected pleasures.

AUTO ABC'S...

When you're driving, use your horn less and your patience more. Running traffic lights, tailgating, and trying to outfox another driver won't really save you time, and it may endanger others around you. Perhaps there should be a refresher course in drivers' education from time to time, along with a checklist of common courtesies.

Your car is for driving, not storing—Keep your car clean of debris, kids' toys, your dry cleaning, and so forth. No one wants to ride in a messy car.

Music—Be congenial and don't impose your music (and the volume) on your passengers.

Sensible stowaways—Maps, tissues or napkins, paper and pen, and bottled water for long trips.

Headlights—Use your bright lights responsibly, not selfishly.

Road rage—Anger management is essential for safe driving, for both you and others. If you become incensed, pull over until you have calmed down.

SUBWAY MOVIES
The Taking of Pelham One, Two, Three (1974)
The Last Metro (1980); *Sliding Doors* (1998)

BINGO!

The telltale green board with its plastic colored sliding windows has been amusing children in cars since 1960, when Auto Bingo (also known as Car Bingo) was first made by Regal Games. Today you can also play Find-a-Car Bingo, Traffic Safety Bingo, and Interstate Highway Bingo.

ETIQUETTE GOES UNDERGROUND—THE SUBWAY

Subway etiquette has its own unique parameters, though being cordial remains the best tactic. Let others get off before entering a subway car; allow one seat per person (that includes any packages as well); if you bump into someone getting on or off the subway, smile and apologize; keep your voice down (ditto for portable musical devices); offer your seat to an older person, someone who is disabled, or a pregnant woman. One other point: a subway car is not a dining car.

AIRPLANE ADVICE

Sharing the armrest and forced conversation are among the irksome social perils of airplane travel. What are your options?

The armrest—One to a customer, and if you're in the center seat, choose one side and stick to it.

Being kicked from behind—For most children, an airplane is even worse than being buckled into the backseat of the family car. If a child is repeatedly kicking the back of your seat, politely speak to the parents.

Making conversation (or not)—Reading a book is enjoyable and sends a signal to the would-be talkative seatmate that you prefer silence to conversation.

The pleasure of your own company—If you really want to sit back and tune out, listen to your portable CD player (with the volume turned down), put on your sunglasses, and sleep.

AIRPLANE MOVIES

Casablanca (1942)
The V.I.P.s (1963)
Goldfinger (1964)
Airplane! (1980)
Love, Actually (2003)

BICYCLING FOR GROWN-UPS

If you're going to ride alongside cars, you need to follow the standard rules of the road.

Obey traffic signs and signals.

Ride with the traffic.

If there's a designated bike lane, use it.

Use proper hand signals when turning and passing.

Ride defensively, and in consideration of your fellow riders. Be on the lookout for potholes and grates, pedestrians and stray animals, cars suddenly stopping and car doors opening. Be smart and wear a whistle around your neck.

Wear a helmet, and don't worry about looking foolish. It's not a beauty contest.

"THE TRUE TRAVELER IS HE WHO GOES ON FOOT,
AND EVEN THEN, HE SITS DOWN A LOT OF THE TIME."

—COLETTE, *PARIS FROM MY WINDOW*

pucci named his wardrobe for braniff airlines' hostesses "air strip" because layers could be removed during flight · 35

VACATION TRAVEL

For the peripatetic, a little trip is always satisfying. The spa retreat, the art excursion, and the gustatory adventure are all worth a timeout from your day to day life.

RESET YOUR WATCH—Get on vacation time and don't bother about the time "back home."

BE IN THE PRESENT—Why talk about the office when you're horseback riding in Aspen?

GOING OVERSEAS?—Make sure your passport is current, and that you arrive at your destination with enough foreign currency to get from the airport to your hotel and buy a coffee and a pastry.

BEFORE THE TRIP YOU WERE THE BEST OF FRIENDS...

If you travel with a friend, plan to take roughly the same amount of luggage; that way neither one of you will potentially slow down the other.

Agree on a budget beforehand.

Discuss your expectations and your privacy preferences.

If things become rocky, realize it's temporary and that sometimes it's wisest to agree to disagree.

Keep a sense of humor!

PARLEZ-VOUS FRANÇAIS?

When you travel to a foreign country, bring your manners with you. What you wear, how long you bathe, even how you address shopkeepers are important. You'll enjoy yourself more when you respect the local customs and do your best to follow them. If you ask for ice water and the waiter adds only a cube or two, don't bemoan it, accept it. Better still, switch to wine.

"SPLENDID MANNERS—IN THE AMERICAN STYLE."
—HENRY JAMES, *PORTRAIT OF A LADY*

AT YOUR HOTEL

Welcome to your home away from home, where the room is always neat, the bed freshly made, and the bathroom squeaky clean. The price for this retreat is a simple understanding of the protocol between you and the staff.

Your hotel concierge is there to make your stay as pleasant as possible and is your primary general contact during your stay. You may rely on him or her to provide you with information and to cheerfully resolve any possible problems. When you ask for special care, be polite and flexible; grandstanding is not only unattractive, it is often self-defeating.

THE HOTEL SOUVENIR

You might think that the hotel ashtray or bath mat would look quaint in your home, but the hotel feels otherwise. Most good hotels, however, will gladly allow you to purchase a signature bathrobe, for example, and they'll be happy to send you home with some bath toiletries and stationery.

PERSONAL PECCADILLOES

Seasoned travelers are not only savvy about the type of room they prefer, they're specific about what they travel with to ratchet up their temporary comfort zones. The range of items is broad (from scented travel candles and pillows to flower vases and little lamp shades), but the selection is always very personal. That said, don't expect the housekeeper to refresh your flowers or clean up spilled candle wax without a personal request and appropriate gratuity.

ROOM 728

If your room is less than ideal, don't ask the bellhop to find you another room (and don't berate him, either). Contact the concierge and discuss your needs. When the bellhop moves you to a more satisfactory room, be sure to double his tip; after all, he has now carried your bags twice.

DRESS ETIQUETTE
FROM MORNING...

"I don't think anyone expects you to be in the same mood seven days
a week, and that goes for how you dress, too. Just the same, I do believe
that certain conventions call out for certain attire. To me, this applies equally to
a major executive or to a young woman working at a little shop. Dressing with
a regard for others is a sign of respect."

"IS MY DESIRE TO DRESS APPROPRIATELY FOR SPECIAL OCCASIONS AS DATED AS A LIME RICKEY?"

OUT AND ABOUT: DRESSING UP, DOWN, AND GOING YOUR OWN WAY

The two pillars of appropriate attire are a true sense of your
own style and an appreciation for the occasion or time of day.

HAIR—Develop a style that best flatters you 24/7. Your hair
should complement, not overwhelm, your appearance.

MAKEUP—It's always fun to buy a new tube of lipstick, but
for daytime keep it simple. A fresh look is an all-around winner.

JEWELRY—When it comes to wearing jewelry during the day,
understatement is the goal unless you are naturally given to
overdrive in your appearance. A couple of choice pieces always
look good.

NAILS—Clean and natural are the operative words here. Anything
else is *de trop* for daytime.

CLOTHES—The ideal wardrobe allows a woman to select clothes
that are suitable for lunch with friends, going to the office, or
doing errands.

...UNTIL NIGHT

"Selecting my wardrobe when Andy and I are headed someplace special is when I get to indulge myself. I love wearing beautiful things and sparkly jewelry, and a night on the town cries out for adornment."

8:00 CURTAIN

Think about where you're going, not just about what you'll be doing. If it's to see La Bohème at the Metropolitan Opera House, make the extra effort. Wear a dress that *radiates*. Remember that lighting in restaurants or at concert halls tends to soften features and add mystery. Dress to thrill.

"AS FAR AS I'M CONCERNED, 'PLAYING DRESS UP' BEGINS AT THE AGE OF FIVE AND NEVER TRULY ENDS."

"Like the elegant décor of the Plaza, the splendor of a theater deserves an audience with attire to match—and I've always been one for matching."

IN A MANNER OF SPEAKING...PUT ON THE DOG

To dress with flair; first used in 1871. "Nothing so delighted Claire and Whit like an evening at the Philharmonic. Claire was resplendent in plumes of coral silk chiffon and Whit put on the dog with his bespoke gray pinstripe suit and Asprey cufflinks."

DRESSING DISASTERS: SLIPS, RIPS, AND BROKEN HEELS

When it comes to dressing, even the best-laid plans can go awry. Just the same, you still have options: be pragmatic, resourceful, and do your best to look upon the incident as *incidental*. Above all, never be self-deprecatory as a way of passing off a sartorial blip.

"Who hasn't had a heel snap or a button burst? Any time you go out, myriad things can go wrong. My advice about the unexpected is pretty simple: laugh, throw back your shoulders, and move on."

A FEW SURPRISES WE'VE ALL EXPERIENCED . . .

The blouse with the missing button—You noticed this during a business lunch. *If you're wearing a blazer, draw it closer; otherwise, pull up your napkin to cover the offending wink of skin.*

A hole in one—You walk into a room, sit down, and realize you've got a large run in your stocking. *Excuse yourself and remove the stockings. Even on a cold day a bare leg is preferable.*

Great dress, wrong bra—When you put on your sleeveless dress it didn't occur to you to check that no straps showed in back. *If you have a shawl or sweater, drape it over your shoulders, or ask a friend to borrow hers.*

You're stepping out of the car and whoops—the heel on your shoe breaks off. *Ask yourself which looks funnier—one bare foot with one shoe, or two bare feet? Sometimes it makes more sense to jettison both shoes.*

The one time you borrow clothes from your best friend, disaster strikes—the zipper breaks, buttons burst, or you become a magnet for mustard. *The sooner you can change, the better. Afterward, be honest and tell your friend what happened; inform her you'll have the garment repaired and dry cleaned. Return it with a short note and a small token expressing your appreciation.*

You missed the fine print: you're the only one in formal wear. *Slip off your jewelry, unpin your hair, and quickly wipe off excess "party" makeup. Then flag down the nearest waiter with the champagne tray.*

You thought the restaurant was casual, when in fact it's dressy, as are all the people already there. *Comb your hair, apply lipstick, and don a confident smile, then glide to your table as though you were in ermine (and pray for a banquette seat). Once the table's pushed in, who will know you're in jeans?*

Your date sees the tags you forgot to remove hanging inside of your new coat. *Laugh it off, then quickly get into your coat and head out the door.*

"HAVE YOU EVER SEEN AN 80-YEAR-OLD WOMAN LOOK GREAT WITH A TATTOO?"

—ANDY SPADE

You thought you were being smart by wearing Band-Aids with your new sandals—until you looked down and saw them poking out. *There's no denying the relief from this little strip of adhesive and gauze, but having your Band-Aids show is not unlike your slip or bra strap showing. Before you go out, make sure they're well tucked away. As backup, it's always smart to carry a few emergency Band-Aids in your wallet.*

SOCIAL SPILLS AND GRACIOUS RECOVERIES

It's one thing to get mail with your last name misspelled and quite another when an acquaintance continually does the same thing (and mispronounces your name as well). What can you do? How can you be gracious without embarrassing your friend?

A FEW SOCIAL SPILLS WE'VE ALL WITNESSED (OR COMMITTED)...

Squirting your seatmate when you crack open a lobster
Offer your bib, if you have one, another napkin, and maybe even a piece of your lobster if it was from the claw.

Arriving a week early for a party
Humor is really the only way out of this one. Explain that you're on a campaign to improve your tardiness and that you seem to have gone slightly overboard in the other direction.

Inquiring after someone's spouse and learning that they're no longer married
It's apparent that this is more of an acquaintance than a close friend, so offer a brief but sincere apology. Don't, however, take license and ask why the marriage ended.

Wearing the same dress as the hostess of an event
This is a case of the Frozen Smile Solution. Doubtless, neither of you is amused by the coincidence, but outwardly make light of it and let it pass.

Spilling a Sea Breeze down the front of your white summer dress
Someone else spilling a Sea Breeze down the front of your white summer dress
Both spills were accidental, and thus it doesn't matter how the cocktail got on your dress. Excuse yourself, find some club soda, and do what you can in the short term to minimize the problem.

And that most unpredictable of bathroom boo-boos: a stubborn toilet
Who said life's fair?

THE NAME GAME

Social faux pas are often committed in the misspelling or mispronunciation of a name. Contrary to the belief that you should grin and bear it, it's actually a kindness to correct the person right then, rather than wait until a later time. Sometimes a delay adds to someone's embarrassment rather than mitigates it. When you do inform someone of your correct name, do so in a friendly and casual manner.

SOME COMMON AND UNCOMMON SPELLINGS

Alice, Alyce	Leah, Lia
Ana, Anna	Lesley, Leslie
Claire, Clare	Lisa, Liza
Eileen, Ilene	LouLou, Lulu
Elise, Elyse	Maira, Maria, Maura, Moira
Elizabeth, Elisabeth, Lisbeth	Sara, Sarah
Joanna, JoAnne	Susan, Suzanne
Karen, Karyn, Caryn	Zoë, Zoey

BLUNDERS...
MISPRONUNCIATION OF A FOREIGN WORD

To the trained ear, it's like fingernails on a blackboard listening to someone mispronounce a foreign word. If you aren't especially facile at foreign languages, opt for the commonly translated title of a film or food (unless of course, *linguini alla vongole* simply sounds better than saying pasta with clams). Also, take care not to salt your words with a bon mot when a good word will work just as well.

WHAT DO YOU DO WHEN...

You're at an interview before a building's co-op board and you get the hiccups?
Ask for some water and try to brush it off by saying you must be a little nervous. If possible, avoid having to excuse yourself from the interview.

You're taking your best friend out for a fancy birthday lunch only to learn after the check arrives that it's cash only—and you have about $20? *You're caught in the middle. You don't want to ask your friend for money, but you can't expect the restaurant to break their rule just for you. However, in a pinch, a restaurant might help you save face if you let them hold your credit card as security while you go to the nearest ATM.*

You've recently arrived in Tokyo for a business trip and you're strolling with important clients when you accidentally step on a wad of gum? *First of all, it's always wise to read up on the customs and manners of a country you'll be visiting. In some cases, England can be as "foreign" to an American as Japan. Lacking any specific information, do your best to ignore the problem until you're somewhere you can excuse yourself and remove the gum in private. (But if you're about to enter someone's home, then you do need to take care of the problem beforehand.)*

You're talking to the company vice president and you realize that his fly is open? *You have a couple of options, and you should select what's most appropriate to your relationship with this person. You can be direct and simply tell him, or you can ignore it and hope some other Good Samaritan will let him know.*

You're at a picnic with a bunch of friends and their children when eight-year-old Sam roughhouses and lands a swift kick to your shin? *Apply ice and grab a beer.*

IN A MANNER OF SPEAKING...
BETWEEN A ROCK AND A HARD PLACE

To be forced to choose between two unsatisfactory
options. A modern variant of the phrase "between
Scylla and Charybdis," from *The Odyssey.* "Lucy was
trying to enjoy herself at a dinner party, but the man
across from her was occasionally kicking her. If she
said something, she risked offending him, but if she
kept quiet, she'd end up with a considerable bruise."

THINGS THAT GO BUMP IN THE NIGHT...

Out of the corner of your eye, you sense movement, or
perhaps you hear a little scratching sound. Maybe there's
no warning; maybe the critter or bug simply appears.
Nothing packs a shot of adrenaline more than discovering
an outdoors animal or insect *indoors.* For the houseguest
who's squeamish or mouse phobic, this is NO FUN.
Mosquitoes, mice, even chipmunks skittering about are best
tolerated and require that you be the Stoic Houseguest, at
least until morning. Then you can decide whether to speak
to your hosts about your night, or write it off to a bad dream.

WHEN STUART LITTLE COMES CALLING...

It's 1 A.M. and you're just about to turn out the light when you see a mouse in
your room. You shriek, the mouse runs, your hosts continue sleeping. Calm
down—the mouse is twenty times more scared than you. The little mouse will
definitely not jump on your covers, though you might want to leave the door
to the hallway open a crack, just in case he wants to go exploring elsewhere.

SECTION TWO

From Me to You:
The Gentle Art of Communicating

Artful Conversation

Telephones, Cell Phones, and Secondhand Chat

Written Correspondence

Invitations, RSVPs, Thank-You Notes

Letters I Love · Letter Trivia

ARTFUL CONVERSATION

"Frankly, I like to talk, so I rarely find myself without something to say. But there is a difference between just *talking* and really thinking about what would interest the other person. Nothing is more embarrassing than possibly boring someone. If I feel stumped when I'm talking with someone, I try to widen the group and pull in more people. Sometimes that's the perfect solution."

"GOOD FENCES MAKE GOOD NEIGHBORS."
—ROBERT FROST, "MENDING WALL"

"Talk to somebody, for Christ's sakes, honey, talk to somebody. If she catches you standing here not talking to anybody, she'll take us off her invitation list, and I love these parties."

—John Cheever,
"The Enormous Radio"

WORDS TO ARTFULLY DODGE...

In mixed company, some words are best left unsaid, such as *short, bald, fat, skinny, still single,* and *unemployed.*

IN A MANNER OF SPEAKING...SPOONERISM

The accidental but often hilarious transposition of initial sounds. The term was named after William A. Spooner, who made many such faux pas. Among his best known: "Son, it is kisstomery to cuss the bride."

SOME TIMELESS ADVICE ON MAKING CONVERSATION

Be a good listener—A sympathetic listener makes others comfortable.

Good conversation is all about give and take—Excel at each.

Being naturally shy is okay—Most of the sins of bad
conversation are made by talking too much, not too little.

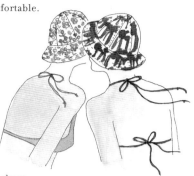

Think before you speak—What's said can't be taken back.

Less is more—No need to tell all.

Silence is acceptable—Don't feel obliged to fill up airtime.

Your age—If you're going to lie, skip the subject altogether.

Think about the topic—Seek common ground and build from there.

Give praise when relevant, but don't go overboard—Too much blunts sincerity and credibility.

Consider what *not* to talk about—Unless you know the person well, it's wiser
to avoid sensitive subjects such as politics, child raising, money, or the Mets.

When talking about your children, easy does it—Touting your
child's skills or appearance can be offputting to your listener.
The same holds true for pets.

The weather—Uniquely boring.

Boasting is boring, too.

Be tactful—Most people don't care to be reminded
about growing older. (Would you?)

Humor is healthy—Sarcasm and malice are not.

Don't worry about being clever—Be genuine, be yourself.

> "CYNICISM IS
> INTELLECTUAL
> DANDYISM, BUT
> GRACIOUSNESS
> IN SPEECH IS AN
> APHRODISIAC."
>
> —ANDY SPADE

PARDON MY FRENCH...

Sugar, *merde!*, drat, crikey, fudge, cor blimey, jiminy
Christmas, balderdash, son of a gun, dang it, for crying out
loud, bull pucky, jiminy cricket, baloney, *schiss, zut alors!*

TELEPHONES, CELL PHONES, AND SECONDHAND CHAT

"I rarely have time for social calls during the day, and we're often out at night, so I try to fit in my phone calling when I'm on my way to a meeting, or perhaps heading out to the airport on a business trip."

HOW TO GIVE GOOD PHONE...

WHEN YOU CALL—Most calls should be placed between 8 A.M. and 10 P.M. on weekdays; 10 A.M. and 10 P.M. on Saturdays; and noon and 10 P.M. on Sundays.

CALL WAITING—Unless you're expecting a call, let the second call go into voice mail. If, however, you decide to answer a call, it should be done only to inform Caller #2 that you will return the call. If you are in the middle of a serious conversation, don't pick up call waiting.

RETURNING CALLS—Personal calls should be returned the same day or within twenty-four hours.

"I'M NOT AFRAID TO ADMIT I LIKE TALKING ON THE PHONE. WEEKENDS ARE BEST OF ALL, WHEN I'M RELAXED AND HAVE A CHANCE TO CATCH UP WITH MY FRIENDS AND MY FAMILY."

CELL PHONE DO'S...

For economy and convenience.

When you're on the go and need to confirm or change appointments, reservations, film schedules.

Keep the conversation friendly.

When you enter a restaurant, a shop, or a museum, set your phone to vibrate; better still, if it's not essential, turn it off.

Children and babysitters—Being reachable is a worthy use of the cell phone.

For an emergency—This goes without saying.

AND DON'TS...

Don't use a cell phone as a panacea for boredom.

Don't use a cell phone to talk in public about personal or professional problems, financial woes, health worries.

Don't swear or conduct an argument on a cell phone in public. Nothing excuses such behavior.

Don't assume it's okay to speak loudly because you think what you're saying is impressive to those around you. Keep your voice low at all times.

Don't assume it's okay to speak at length while on a train or in an airplane.

Deep-six cell phones
in restaurants.

SECONDHAND CHAT

Secondhand chat is right up there with secondhand smoke. By the time you've finished looking in a boutique, chances are that if someone is on a cell phone, you'll wind up knowing her shoe size, what she's shopping for, and her budget. You'll probably even know the name of her date. This is selfish and boring. Please, don't blow smoke in our face or talk in our ear.

CELL HELL

"I have a like/dislike relationship with my cell phone. The ease and freedom it gives are great, but like a lot of people, I'm not used to being 'connected' so frequently. When people use cell phones in public, such as on the street, while shopping, or in a doctor's office, I wish they would use more discretion and be considerate of others around them."

WRITTEN CORRESPONDENCE

"I love stationery, so I can never have enough beautiful writing papers around. If I were a lady of leisure, I'd find it peaceful to spend my mornings at a proper writing desk, sending off little notes to people. As it is, I never have that kind of morning (or day, for that matter). Who doesn't enjoy receiving a note in the mail?"

LETTERS

"You deserve a longer letter than this; but it is my unhappy fate seldom to treat people so well as they deserve."

—Jane Austen

FORMAL SALUTATIONS

We may live in a more casual society, but a little decorum is still called for in proper letters. It never hurts to err on the side of politesse, and if you think you should use a surname in a thank-you letter, then begin your note with the salutation "Ms.," "Mrs.," or "Mr." Switch to a first-name basis once you have established a mutual rapport.

"ALWAYS HANDWRITE A FORMAL SOCIAL NOTE."

NEATNESS COUNTS

Not all penmanship is created equal, but you can control the overall look of a letter. Spilled coffee, a bent piece of paper, and words crossed out are all telltale indications of a letter best left unsent. For the recipient, the appearance of your letter is a stand-in for you.

"DO NOT BE TEMPTED BY A TWENTY-DOLLAR WORD WHEN THERE IS A TEN-CENTER HANDY, READY, AND ABLE."

—WILLIAM STRUNK, JR., AND E. B. WHITE, *THE ELEMENTS OF STYLE*

Nowadays, house stationery is a restitution of more traditional times. Some people choose to have house stationery if they own a second, or country, home.

BE NATURAL

For personal correspondence use natural language and avoid sounding mannered or formal. Feel free to use contractions, such as *it's* and *I'm*, which echo our everyday speech.

IN A MANNER OF SPEAKING...CLICHÉS

There are scores of clichés from all over the world, and many of them have as their source either the Bible or Shakespeare. It's easy as pie to use a cliché, but in correspondence, remember that a little goes a long way, so take the following phrases with a pinch of salt: two peas in a pod; dancing on the head of a pin; bib and tucker; grin like a Cheshire cat; knock the socks off; two left feet; birds of a feather flock together; and life is a bowl of cherries.

"BREVITY IS THE SOUL OF WIT."

—SHAKESPEARE

ENVELOPE SIZES	
ENVELOPE	SIZE
A2	$4^{3}/_{8}$ by $5^{3}/_{4}$"
A6	$4^{3}/_{4}$ by $6^{1}/_{2}$"
A7	$5^{1}/_{4}$ by $7^{1}/_{4}$"
A8	$5^{1}/_{2}$ by $8^{1}/_{8}$"
A10	6 by $9^{1}/_{2}$"
$6^{1}/_{4}$"	$3^{1}/_{2}$ by 6"
$6^{3}/_{4}$"	$3^{5}/_{8}$ by $6^{1}/_{2}$"
$7^{3}/_{4}$"	$3^{7}/_{8}$ by $7^{1}/_{2}$"
$8^{5}/_{8}$"	$3^{5}/_{8}$ by $8^{5}/_{8}$"
9"	$3^{7}/_{8}$ by $8^{7}/_{8}$"
10"	$4^{1}/_{8}$ by $9^{1}/_{2}$"
11"	$4^{1}/_{2}$ by $10^{3}/_{8}$"

PAPER SIZES	
PAPER	SIZE
MONARCH	$7^{1}/_{4}$ x $10^{1}/_{2}$"
HALF	$5^{1}/_{4}$ x $3^{3}/_{4}$"
BUSINESS	$8^{1}/_{2}$ x 11"
LETTER	$5^{1}/_{4}$ x $7^{1}/_{2}$"
CHIT	$5^{3}/_{8}$ x $4^{1}/_{8}$"
POSTCARD	4 x 6"

IN A MANNER OF SPEAKING...BROWNIE POINTS

Indicating favor or kudos. "Hallie had always been a reliable correspondent, but she earned brownie points from her parents for the frequent and endearing letters she sent them while in the south of France. Perhaps it was the sea air."

GREAT DIARISTS

Dr. Johnson

Anne Frank

Samuel Pepys

Katharine Graham

Tibor Kalman

Henry Stimson

Cecil Beaton

Eleanor Roosevelt

Virginia Woolf

Andy Warhol

Bridget Jones

"I HAVE MADE THIS LETTER LONGER, BECAUSE
I HAVE NOT HAD THE TIME TO MAKE IT SHORTER."

—BLAISE PASCAL

CORRESPONDENCE THAT
NEVER GOES OUT OF STYLE

General invitations

Wedding invitations

Birth announcements

Place cards

Thank-you notes

"Dear John" letters

Love letters

Vacation postcards

Fan mail

Moving or new home announcements

THE STATIONERY WARDROBE

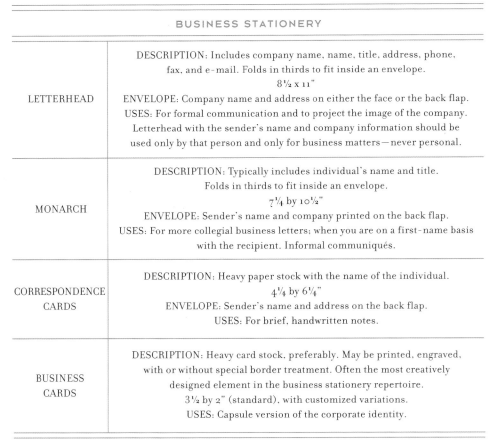

"when we began our company, we were so small (there were just four of us and not that many handbags) that we decided all of our correspondence should be lowercase as a reflection of our size. whether a letter was typed, whether it was someone's name or the beginning of a sentence, we used lowercase. we took it very seriously. i suppose we've grown up because now we use uppercase and lowercase."

BUSINESS STATIONERY

LETTERHEAD	DESCRIPTION: Includes company name, name, title, address, phone, fax, and e-mail. Folds in thirds to fit inside an envelope. 8½ x 11" ENVELOPE: Company name and address on either the face or the back flap. USES: For formal communication and to project the image of the company. Letterhead with the sender's name and company information should be used only by that person and only for business matters—never personal.
MONARCH	DESCRIPTION: Typically includes individual's name and title. Folds in thirds to fit inside an envelope. 7¼ by 10½" ENVELOPE: Sender's name and company printed on the back flap. USES: For more collegial business letters; when you are on a first-name basis with the recipient. Informal communiqués.
CORRESPONDENCE CARDS	DESCRIPTION: Heavy paper stock with the name of the individual. 4¼ by 6¼" ENVELOPE: Sender's name and address on the back flap. USES: For brief, handwritten notes.
BUSINESS CARDS	DESCRIPTION: Heavy card stock, preferably. May be printed, engraved, with or without special border treatment. Often the most creatively designed element in the business stationery repertoire. 3½ by 2" (standard), with customized variations. USES: Capsule version of the corporate identity.

Ways to close a business letter: *Sincerely; Sincerely yours; Very truly yours; Yours truly; Gratefully*

SOCIAL STATIONERY

LETTER SHEETS	DESCRIPTION: Name and address, or only address. Folds in half to fit inside an envelope. ENVELOPE: Name and address, or only address. USES: For more general correspondence or for a lengthy note.
FOLD-OVER NOTES	DESCRIPTION: So called because they fold along the left side or top. May be printed or engraved with your full name, a monogram, or one initial on the cover page. Write on pages 1, 3, and 2, in that order. The back side should remain blank. Folds in half to fit inside an envelope. $5\frac{1}{4}$ by $7\frac{1}{2}$" ENVELOPE: Name and address, or only address. USES: The most formal of social stationery. As a reply to a formal invitation, sympathy note.
HALF-SHEET	DESCRIPTION: Named because they are half the size of a letter sheet. May have only a name, a name and address, or be monogrammed. The second sheet is unembellished. $5\frac{1}{4}$ by $3\frac{3}{4}$" ENVELOPE: Name and address, or only address. USES: For general correspondence.
CORRESPONDENCE CARDS (also known as "informals")	DESCRIPTION: More informal than a letter but regarded as the principal form of social stationery. Heavy card stock, with optional monogramming or name across the top. May be plain or bordered. No fold. Write only on the front side. $6\frac{3}{4}$ x $4\frac{1}{4}$" ENVELOPE: Address on two lines on back of envelope. USES: The most versatile of all social stationery—as a thank-you note, or turned into an invitation, or stamped and sent as a postcard.
CALLING CARDS	DESCRIPTION: Heavy paper stock. May include only the name, name and phone, or the name and address. The address is typically in the lower right-hand corner. $2\frac{7}{8}$ by 2" (if single) or $3\frac{1}{8}$ by $2\frac{1}{4}$" (if married) USES: Mainly as gift enclosures or for social purposes.

Ways to close a social letter: *Warmly; Warm regards; Best; Fondly; Affectionately; Appreciatively; Yours*

BUSINESS LETTERS

Traditionally, every business letter was typed. Nowadays, formal communication should be typed. Be sure to always include the addressee's name and full title, in addition to the company name and address.

TYPE/WRITER

When is a business letter written by hand? To thank your department head or boss for a Sunday outing or for helping with something at the office. Although the handwriting suggests a more casual relationship, the language and tone of your note should remain professional.

Timely correspondence is key to maintaining healthy and active professional relationships.

BUSINESSESE IS A FOREIGN LANGUAGE

Be direct and use plain language; keep to the point; be specific; use active verbs; state your expectations of the recipient; be professional, be human.

WINDBAG WORDS

Some language and phrases are inherently clunky, obtuse, or deadly dull. Do your best to avoid the following . . .

Enclosed herewith
Here is

Due to the fact that
Because

Per your request/Further to your request
As you mentioned

As to when/Until such time
When

REPETITIVE REDUNDANCIES

Final conclusion

Mix together

Basic fundamentals

Specifically customized

Very urgent

Very unique (now, that is special!)

"I DON'T WRITE MANY FORMAL LETTERS, BUT ANYTHING WITH MY SIGNATURE IS ALWAYS HANDWRITTEN."

E-MAIL AND FAXES

"I'm a Luddite when it comes to e-mail. I love writing letters too much to think that e-mail should be anything but a convenience. But of course I understand its usefulness at work."

E-mail is so easy and fast that it's possible to overlook the courtesies naturally associated with more conventional forms of communication.

IN THE OFFICE—E-mail should always be professional, regardless of the brevity or frequency of your correspondence with another colleague. The "send" button is powerful: don't send an e-mail when you're angry. Be discreet: any e-mails sent within a company may be forwarded to others, and may also be reviewed at any time by management.

AT HOME—As with any personal correspondence, remember that your character is represented by what you write. Don't waste other people's time by forwarding a joke or graphic to everyone in your address book. If you're upset or angry, then e-mail is best avoided, for you and the recipient.

> "EVERYBODY GETS SO MUCH INFORMATION ALL DAY LONG THAT THEY LOSE THEIR COMMON SENSE."
>
> —GERTRUDE STEIN

While the fax machine beats snail mail in terms of speed, bear in mind a few pointers:

Sending a confidential fax is inherently risky, so take necessary precautions.

Never read a fax intended for someone else.

Don't send pages and pages of a document by fax unless cleared beforehand with the recipient; it can tie up or jam a machine. (Consider a messenger, express mail, or e-mail.)

Time of day—The safest time to fax is daytime, yours and the recipient's. Never send a fax during the night to someone's home.

INVITATIONS

"Andy and I love to give parties, and whether they're casual gatherings or big blowouts, half the fun is creating the invitation. I love the formal presentation of a proper invitation, and Andy always helps with the imagery and the words. His injections of humor are priceless."

"IF YOU MUST INVITE A CHATTERBOX, TRY TO DILUTE HER WITH COMPANY."

—ANONYMOUS

Invitations are usually written in the third person
and are best sent two weeks ahead of time.

WHEN YOU SEND AN INVITATION,
please be sure to add all the essentials:

Event

Date

Time

Place

Style of dress, if relevant

RSVP

If an occasion is informal, then you can phone your friends, though in the end you may find it's not the best way to keep careful tabs on everyone. *Bear in mind: never issue an invitation to someone in front of others, and once you have extended invites, they should be recalled for only the most compelling of reasons.*

IN A MANNER OF SPEAKING . . . FIELD DAY

To have an enjoyable time. The phrase derives from the time when circuses and fairs typically set up in fields. "Although secretly she'd dreaded turning forty, Ruby had a field day at the party her close friends gave. The Japanese hanging lanterns, the scent of wisteria, and Bellinis were all such thoughtful, personal touches."

RSVPS

This is one French expression that just about everyone who has ever gone to a special event knows. In the world of etiquette, it's right up there with *please* and *thank you*.

WHEN AN RSVP IS UNNECESSARY

Formal or informal invitations to cocktail parties or teas don't require an acceptance unless an RSVP is included. For these events, many hostesses may even indicate "regrets only" as a way of keeping a rough head count.

Among close friends, it's fine to call and RSVP to an informal event or holiday gathering.

A CARD LAID IS A CARD PLAYED

The decision to accept or reject an invitation is yours, but once you do accept, you must honor your obligation to the host. Nothing excuses breaking one commitment so that you can attend another event. (It would be very embarrassing if word got back to the original host that your "headache" had cleared and you were seen at another party.)

A reply to a formal invitation should be made within two days.

WHEN YOU ACCEPT—Repeat the event, date, and time.

WHEN YOU DECLINE—Repeat the event and date, and include a brief reason for your regret.

THANK-YOU NOTES

"Thank-you notes make all the difference between *feeling* grateful and *showing* your gratitude. You're not a bad person if you don't send off a note of thanks, and certainly I understand how busy everyone is, but I do believe that it's better to send the card than to agonize over not having warmly thanked someone."

When you send a note, refer to the actual gift, event, or even the conversation that you're acknowledging.

The "Three-Day Rule" applies to sending a thank-you note as well as responding to a written invitation with an RSVP.

"THE WORST INDIGNITY DOES NOT EXCUSE YOU FROM WRITING A DELIRIOUS LETTER THANKING YOUR HOSTESS FOR A *HEAVENLY* WEEK-END."

—ALICE-LEONE MOATS

"Dear Judith and Evan: This is an unpardonable time for a b&b . . . not to mention a few other Common Courtesies like saving my reason if not my life when I could not get across Third and 50th. I know you understand my laxness. Whether you condone it is another matter. . . ."

—To Judith and Evan Jones,
May 29, 1971, from M.F.K. Fisher

IN A MANNER OF SPEAKING . . . A BREAD-AND-BUTTER LETTER
A note of thanks acknowledging someone's hospitality, originally following a weekend as a houseguest. "Amy meant to send off a bread-and-butter letter right away thanking Meg for the marathon tennis weekend, but what with the two babies and new home, she was a week or so behind." Better late than never.

CHILDREN AND THANK-YOU NOTES

Until a child can make some scribbles of his or her own, thank-you notes should come from you. But please, write on behalf of your child, not in the first person as your child, which only moves the dial from cute to cutesy. Around the age of five or so, however, encourage your child to write a sentence or two. Don't worry about the results; the recipient will be charmed by the wayward handwriting and whatever is written. Over time, the act of sending a note will take root; expect full growth by the age of fourteen.

Sometimes just the words *thank you* and a bottle of wine send the perfect message.

"An engraved or printed thank-you card, no matter how attractive its design, cannot take the place of a personally written message of thanks."

—Emily Post

THE TARDY THANK-YOU NOTE

It happens: even with the best of intentions, your note is weeks late. What to do? Write it and send it along anyway. You may need to be a bit clever in your note, but there is no need to belabor its tardiness. Concentrate on the gift or affair itself. As with any note of this kind, be sincere.

LETTERS I LOVE

"Great letter writing is an art that I admire and which I hope never disappears, especially with so many more people sending faxes and e-mail. A courtship in letters is priceless, and a letter with wit is an achievement."

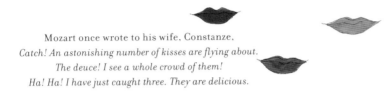

Mozart once wrote to his wife, Constanze,
Catch! An astonishing number of kisses are flying about.
The deuce! I see a whole crowd of them!
Ha! Ha! I have just caught three. They are delicious.

John Lennon was awarded an MBE (Member of the Order of the British Empire), which he initially accepted and later turned down, for political reasons. His telegram to Queen Elizabeth:

Your Majesty, I am returning this MBE in protest against Britain's involvement in the Nigeria-Biafra scene, against our support of America in Vietnam and against Cold Turkey slipping down the charts.

With love, John Lennon

Zelda Sayre to F. Scott Fitzgerald,
Spring 1919:

Don't you think I was made for you? I feel like you had me ordered—and I was delivered to you—to be worn—I want you to wear me, like a watch—charm or a button hole bouquet—to the world.

Letter from Jack Kerouac to Joyce Johnson, June 27, 1957:

Dear Joyce, Disregard last letter. I think exaggerated conditions here in gloomy mood.... Go ahead as planned, I'll be with you all the way...all the way to Mexico, eventually, I have an idea...and you must write a novel about Mexico too!

Love
Jack

Letters between Winston Churchill and his wife, Clementine, are valuable for the insight they give us into their 57-year marriage and as a record of a remarkable time in history. Hers was written in 1909, and his in August 1914.

My Darling

I gave the P.K. her bath to-night—Hodgy Podgy says I did it quite nicely & I want to do it always now, & she, H.P., is quite jealous—

I have found a lovely new ride for us on Saturday—

I hope you will have a nice dinner party to-night—I do wish I was there. . . .

Good-night my darling Pug—I must have lessons in Kat-drawing as your pugs are so much better than my Kats

Your loving
Clementine

Cat—dear—

It is all up. Germany has quenched the last hopes of peace by declaring war on Russia, & the decla-ration against France is momentarily expected.

I profoundly understand your views—But the world is gone mad—& we must look after ourselves—& our friends. It wd be good of you to come for a day or two next week. I miss you much—Your influence when guiding & not contrary is of the utmost use to me.

Sweet Kat—my tender love—

Your devoted
W

Kiss the kittens

David O. Selznick was one of the all-time great Hollywood producers (*Dinner at Eight, A Star Is Born, Gone With the Wind*) and was famous for his prodigious correspondence on matters large and small. The telegram is from Selznick to Katharine Brown, of Selznick International, in 1939, regarding Ingrid Bergman in the forthcoming *Intermezzo,* her first American-made film:

I NOTE BERGMAN IS 69¼ INCHES TALL. IS IT POSSIBLE SHE IS ACTUALLY THIS HIGH, AND DO YOU THINK WE WILL HAVE TO USE STEPLADDERS WITH LESLIE HOWARD?

Letter from E. B. White in 1951 to the head of the ASPCA, who had accused him of not paying taxes on his dog in Maine:

You asked about Minnie's name, sex, breed, and phone number. She doesn't answer the phone. She is a dachshund and can't reach it, but she wouldn't answer it even if she could, as she has no interest in outside calls.

When the humorist Robert Benchley visited Venice for the first time, he sent a friend the following telegram:

STREETS FULL OF WATER.
PLEASE ADVISE.

Telegram from F. Scott Fitzgerald
to Zelda Fitzgerald, 1920

James Thurber's drawings and stories delighted readers of *The New Yorker* for years. As it turns out, his personal letters were also a revelation of wit and heart, as is this one to his daughter, Rosemary, in 1947:

Pansies have always been one of my favorite flowers and I shall put this one between the pages of the album containing your baby pictures, including the one of you strangling the snake which made us think that you were going to turn out to be the first woman president of the United States. . . . Helen and I are delighted by the increase in your correspondence and the darn swell letters you write. What are you trying to do, be better than me?

Love and kisses from us both.
Daddy

Telegram from Harpo Marx to then Senator John F. Kennedy, congratulating Kennedy on receiving the Democratic nomination for president, July 1960:

FIRST—CONGRATULATIONS.
SECOND—DO YOU NEED A HARP PLAYER IN YOUR CABINET.
THIRD—MY BEST TO YOUR MA AND PA.

John Donne to Sir Henry Wotton:

Sir, more than kisses,

Letters mingle souls;

For, thus absent friends speak.

With his customary droll humor, S. J. Perelman replied to a young designer who had sent him a fan letter but had misspelled his name:

The next time you issue a demand for anything, honey, whether it's a spoonful of farina or a Christmas card, examine the name of the person you're asking and spell it correctly. Now wipe the egg off your face and have a happy New Year.

LETTER TRIVIA

"Like so many girls, I had a pen pal when I was a teenager, and I was always thrilled to get mail. My sisters and I were also pulled into writing chain letters, which probably got us into the habit of what is now called correspondence. And though I'm not a serious stamp collector, I do think it's a wonderful hobby, and I love when Andy picks up the occasional old stamp with flowers on it at the flea market."

"DEAR JOHN"

Not every romance survived the prolonged separation when men went off to fight in World War II. For the woman who had chosen to leave the marriage, the news was conveyed to her overseas serviceman by letter. "John" was the name for any soldier (going back to the refrain in a song from 1917, "Over There").

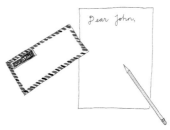

WATERMARKS

A watermark is typically a discreet indication of the maker of the stationery. It is translucent in effect and most visible when held up to the light. Over its seven-hundred-year history, the watermark has been a symbolic way of encoding a message, proprietary (a papal cross, a crown), or a reference to the quality of the paper used. Today, a watermark is centered toward the bottom of a sheet of paper, though it was originally centered in the body of the paper. A watermark may be letters or numerals, be geometric, or depict a scene.

"DEAR CLASSMATES"

The 1903 graduating class of Goucher College, in Baltimore, participated in a fifty-year round-robin of letter writing. More than 35 women from a class of 54 wrote to one another about marriage and children, education, work, both world wars, the depression, travel, and getting older.

FETCH!

More than 100 dog breeds have been featured on stamps
in countries all over the world. For would-be collectors
and dog fanciers, that's a lot of letters to fetch.

Bernese Mountain Dog—Ajman, Bhutan

Border Collie—New Zealand

Borzoi—Abkhazia and Buriatia, both in Russia

French Bulldog—Bhutan

Irish Water Spaniel—Ireland

King Charles Spaniel—Great Britain

Scottish Terrier—Antigua and Barbuda

IN A MANNER OF SPEAKING...CATCH-22

Of the many phrases and sayings that abound, this one has a relatively young but literary
pedigree. Joseph Heller coined the phrase in his novel by the same name in 1961. Then, as now,
it indicated a dilemma in which the choice creates another problem, equally unsatisfactory.
"Barbara was seriously crazy about chocolate, and her latest passion was tiny dark chocolate
nuggets. Now she was down to her last six, and that was always the catch-22: eating them
was a delicious proposition, but if she ate them all, then she wouldn't have any left to eat."

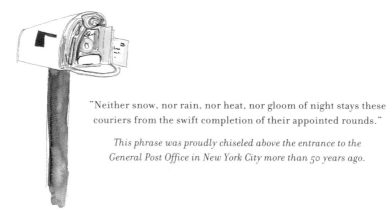

"Neither snow, nor rain, nor heat, nor gloom of night stays these
couriers from the swift completion of their appointed rounds."

*This phrase was proudly chiseled above the entrance to the
General Post Office in New York City more than 50 years ago.*

IN SCRABBLE, LANGUAGE IS AN EIGHT-LETTER WORD, UP, DOWN, OR SIDEWAYS

JAZY—The highest score for a four-letter word. It means "a worsted wig" and at face value is worth 23 points.

ETAERIO—The most likely seven-letter word to appear on the game rack. It means "an aggregate fruit."

An enterprising architect named Alfred Butts devised this word game in 1948 as a way to combine vocabulary skills and chance. He called it Criss-Cross Words, but with his partner changed it to Scrabble, which means "to grope frantically." Of the many rules and important terms for Scrabble players to know, perhaps the most damning is "coffeehousing," which means distracting your opponent from the play at hand. This is strictly forbidden.

SOME KEY DATES...

1450 Gutenberg prints his massive Bible

1638 First printing press set up in America, in Cambridge, Mass.

1780 Earliest use of the steel-nib pen

1798 Invention of lithography

1847 First postage stamps in America

1868 The typewriter is patented

1880 Invention of monotype and linotype

INTRODUCING MR. ZIP...

On July 1, 1963 the U.S. Post Office introduced Mr. Zip to the American public. Mr. Zip's surname is an acronym for Zone Improvement Plan.

MOVIES AND LETTERS

The Postman Always Rings Twice—
Lana Turner, John Garfield

The Scarlet Letter—
Lillian Gish, Lars Hanson

The Letter—
Bette Davis, Herbert Marshall

Cyrano de Bergerac—
Gérard Depardieu, Anne Brochet

Shakespeare in Love—
Gwyneth Paltrow, Joseph Fiennes

You've Got Mail—
Tom Hanks, Meg Ryan

QWERTY SKILLS

The longest words that can be typed with the left hand
are *desegregated, reverberated, stewardesses, watercress.*

The longest words that can be typed with the right hand
are *homophony, nonillion, pollinium, polyphony.*

The longest word than can be typed on the top row is *rupturewort;*
and the longest words from the middle row are *Hadassah* and *alfalfa.*

SECTION THREE

A Manners Miscellany

BOB & CAROL & TED & ALICE

MAKING INTRODUCTIONS—For every matchmaker, there's someone else who thinks fate should do the introductions. If you're a "people" person, someone who enjoys being with people and introducing others, then follow your natural inclination. But once you've introduced a man and a woman, it's best to remove yourself. Otherwise, that all-too-knowing expression "shoot the messenger" might be applied to you.

SWAK—Does anyone know what a first date is anymore? Maybe not, but one thing is unchanged, and that's a kiss. Whether you've been taken to a four-star French restaurant or you've gone together to a bookstore and then out for coffee, there is no rule that says your date must be sealed with a kiss. Or even with an air kiss, or just a handshake.

THE PAST IS PROLOGUE, NOT DIALOGUE—It's a slippery slope when either person on a date talks about an ex. Stay in the present, look to the future.

"I LOVE MICKEY MOUSE MORE THAN ANY WOMAN I HAVE EVER KNOWN."

—WALT DISNEY

IN A MANNER OF SPEAKING...THE BEE'S KNEES

The best, or of high quality, derived from the fact that when bees carry pollen, it's in little sacs on their legs. "What more could she ask for? He sent flowers, they had a weekend of marathon movies, he dressed well, and he was funny. In sum, and as far as Donna was concerned, Tom was the bee's knees."

ALL IN THE FAMILY

HOLIDAYS—For the half-dozen or so times a family gets together to celebrate a holiday, it's incumbent on everyone to be on their best behavior. These are the occasions when you can look around the room and appreciate that of the hundreds of people you know, this group is the nearest to your heart and the people who care most about you.

COMMON COURTESIES—Among the members of your family, don't make the mistake of assuming that you can be late without phoning ahead, cancel a visit, or borrow something without asking (even your mother's pruning shears).

WET TOWELS—Sharing the bathroom is sort of adorable when children are small and you can control how many times they hop in and out of the tub. After that, the bathroom can become territory even Napoleon could covet. Who likes stepping on a soggy bathmat? Or finding someone else's wet towel on your dry one? Like every common room in the home, this is one place where continual courtesies are always appreciated.

THIS, TOO, SHALL PASS—Warfare in the form of sibling rivalry is first learned at home, some of it physical (two brothers playing swords); some of it mental (a sister outfoxing her brother for the last piece of cake); and some of it hierarchical (the oldest gets first use of the family car but is expected to pick up the younger ones at school). Blessedly, most of these childhood torments fall away after adolescence and result in familial friendships. As the parent, practice patience and bear in mind that this, too, shall pass.

"A FAMILY IS A UNIT COMPOSED NOT ONLY OF
CHILDREN BUT OF MEN, WOMEN, AN OCCASIONAL
ANIMAL, AND THE COMMON COLD."

—OGDEN NASH

IN A MANNER OF SPEAKING . . . BLACK SHEEP

To be regarded as the renegade or outcast. Long ago, shepherds believed that black sheep frightened the white sheep in the herd, hence they were cast out of the flock. "No matter how you looked at it, Julian was the black sheep of the family: of the three boys, he was the one who stayed out past his curfew, lost his allowance (or spent it too quickly), and was late coming to the table for dinner most nights. Just the same, to his mother he was a darling."

SOCIAL GRACES, MINOR ANNOYANCES

MAY I AIR-KISS YOU? The handshake of yesterday is the air kiss of today. If you'd rather shake hands, then be swift and extend your hand in greeting before someone leans over to plant a kiss. Depending on where you live, the social air kiss can vary: in some cities, one kiss will do it; in others it's European style, with a buss to both sides. If you each turn so that you accidentally kiss on the lips, make light of it.

TO HUG OR NOT TO HUG—If you're friends, then yes. If it's a business colleague or client, with whom there is a genuine rapport, then yes. If you're meeting up with a group that includes good friends and near-acquaintances, then hugging everyone is optional—but so time-consuming!

SORRY, BUT WHAT'S YOUR NAME?—You're in a swoon, you and your new amour kiss, and he calls you by someone else's name. What to do—step on his foot? Vow never to go out with him again? Or call him by a wrong name? If you care, then bring it to his attention, but don't let it keep you up at night.

WE MUST DO LUNCH

Sincerity is the cornerstone of good manners, so if you suggest lunch or a drink to someone, be sure to mean it. Follow up with a phone call or written invite within two days' time.

BYOP—You've just settled down into your seat for a movie and dug into your popcorn, which . . . is greasy and stale. And cost you $7, thank you very much. Should you get up and go back on line? No, but next time bring your own.

DOUBLE DIPPING—It's not sanitary, it's certainly not appetizing to witness, yet just about everybody does it. If you're passing hors d'oeuvres, you can help prevent this by immediately offering someone a napkin or toothpick. You can't reform all of the folks all of the time, but no harm comes from trying.

THE CELL PHONE REDUX—Don't use the availability of a friend or colleague on her cell phone as an excuse for being late for a date or an appointment.

THE ART OF THE TOOTHPICK
Actually, there is no art to using a toothpick. When you feel the need for a little dentistry, excuse yourself and take care of the problem in private.

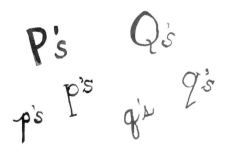

IN A MANNER OF SPEAKING . . . MIND YOUR P'S AND Q'S
To be on your best behavior and mindful of your language. When all type was set by hand, typesetters needed to be particularly careful not to confuse their *p*'s with their *q*'s. "Tim, who was known to guffaw at the most inappropriate of times, did his best to mind his p's and q's when visiting his conservative godparents."

TARDINESS—Some people are inherently tardy, no matter how hard they try; others are always early. With understanding, both kinds of people can be accommodated. What isn't excusable, however, is calling someone at the exact time you're supposed to meet and saying that you'll be anywhere from 15 to 30 minutes late. Calling ahead shows respect for the other person.

SAMPLE SALES—Everybody loves a bargain, and for the Constant Shopper, a sample sale is right up there next to heaven. But don't let this feeding frenzy make *you* frenzied. Tugging and pulling, and griping and glaring are beneath you. After all, just because a two-ply cashmere sweater in your favorite color has been reduced from $395 to $125, doesn't mean that you should have it. Or does it?

WHISPERING, GOSSIPING, AND YELLING

Whispering once or twice in a movie or during a performance is justifiable, and yelling on a baseball field is also understandable. But gossiping is as reckless as riding in a car without a seat belt. Buckle up, button up, zip it, sshhhh.

IN A MANNER OF SPEAKING . . . MAD MONEY

Money that a lady carries should the date end in a quarrel (Webster's, 1922). "Dianne had long been trained to carry around a little mad money with her, just in case something went wonky on a date. But she hadn't expected that would ever happen when she was out with John. Alas, it did."

MANICURES ON THE GO—Some habits die hard, such as filing or clipping one's nails in public, and yet nothing is more inappropriate. On a long bus ride, while sitting on a park bench, or (heaven forbid!) while waiting for your date in a restaurant are all manicure no-no's. When it comes to lavishing care on your hands and feet, please visit a nail salon, or do your beautifying at home.

IT'S NOT MUSIC TO MY EARS—If it's your portable CD player, a few reminders will prevent others from wanting to pull the plug, so to speak. When you're at the beach, consider that the couple reading ten yards away prefers the sound of the waves to the sound of your hip-hop. At the office, follow company protocol. If playing music is acceptable and considered inspiring, be considerate of your coworkers and adjust the volume. If playing music is frowned upon during the day, then save your tunes for after-hours work.

TO ERR IS HUMAN,
TO FORGIVE DIVINE.

GUM IS Y/GUMMY

A piece of gum is refreshing and a quick fix if you're hungry, thirsty, or bored. In public, please don't smack your chops, blow bubbles, or snap your gum when you chew. And if you're with others, then offer gum all around. Of course some circumstances are inherently gum free, such as a job interview, baby christening, or romantic dinner for two.

UNGRACIOUS GIGGLES

"My church giggles grew louder and louder, and the more I tried to tame them, the worse they got, until the Church of England must have had doubts about my prospects for salvation."
—Sarah Ferguson

HOSPITALITY AND FOOD

MAKE MINE A BAGEL WITH COFFEE—If you're having
family or friends for the weekend, especially if they're from
out of town, be thoughtful and ask if there are special food
requests. In particular, most people have a set routine
when it comes to breakfast and they'll be grateful if you
can accommodate them.

THE INTOXICATED GUEST—"A girlfriend of Kate's stayed
up late with us one evening and we all decided it would be a
good idea for her to spend the night. I gave her one of my
T-shirts, a toothbrush, water, and said good-night. When
we woke the next morning she was gone, leaving a thank-
you note with apologies. A few days later she sent a package.
Inside was a T-shirt printed with the words *inebriated guest
T-shirt for sleeping over.*" —Andy Spade

I have eaten
the plums
that were in
the icebox

and which
you were probably
saving
for breakfast

Forgive me
they were delicious
so sweet
and so cold

—William Carlos Williams,
"This Is Just to Say"

"HERE'S YOUR HAT, WHAT'S YOUR HURRY."
—OLD AMERICAN SAYING

IN A MANNER OF SPEAKING...DUTCH TREAT

Paying your own way. From the seventeenth century, when the
Dutch were regarded by the English as their rivals. ("Going Dutch"
is an Americanism, dating to 1914.) "For all the years they'd been
friends, Sophie and Sarah went Dutch treat when it came to
dining out. It simplified the whole who-pays-for-what dilemma."

IN A MANNER OF SPEAKING...GRATUITY

Meaning graciousness or favor. From the French *gratuité* or
medieval Latin *gratuitas* for "thankful." "Susan and Adrian
were regulars at their corner French bistro, where they
liked to bring their own wine. The waiters never minded,
although a supplemental gratuity was added to their bill."

WHAT'S MINE IS MINE

ON LENDING AND BORROWING BOOKS—It's been six
months since a newish friend has borrowed a book of yours.
Can you ask for it back without seeming impolite or embarrassing the friend?
Yes. It's never wrong to ask for what is yours. However, if someone asks to
borrow a book that you care about, then you're better off suggesting some
other book instead.

LENDING CLOTHES—In gambling, the token guideline is that you should
never gamble what you can't afford to lose. Ditto when it comes to your clothes.
If you're the borrower, make sure to have the garment cleaned after wearing
and return it to its owner, preferably in better condition than you received it,
and within a week's time.

OFFICE MATES—Although a friend or colleague would never come into your
home and walk off with your dictionary or calculator, trespasses of this nature
occur in offices with surprising frequency. And with no discernible sign of
embarrassment, either. The rules of borrowing still apply: don't take anything
without asking. Everyone has a favorite something, even if it's only a pencil.

HOME LOANS

It's Friday night, you've packed the car
with groceries, your swimsuit, and the dog,
and you're headed to the country house.
Someone else's country house. When
friends graciously lend you the use of their
home, take care not to overstep your
boundaries in their absence. Don't assume
you can cut their lilacs and put them in your
room or run the air conditioner willy-nilly.
Ask them for any guidelines before
you arrive, and remember, what's theirs
remains theirs, even in absentia.

GIFTS, GIFTING, RE-GIFTING

"RE-GIFTING IS AN ART FORM. BUT
BEWARE: IF YOU RE-GIFT TO OTHERS,
THEY MAY RE-GIFT UNTO YOU."

—ANDY SPADE

WHEN THE GIFT'S NOT RIGHT—Nothing is ever to be gained from parsing the truth, but flat-out honesty isn't always the best solution, either, when you've received a gift that doesn't fit, isn't your style, or would look out of place in your home. The grin-and-bear-it approach works only some of the time. What if, for example, the gift is a dress that is overly tight, or yards too big? Step up to the plate and offer a warm thanks. And depending on the relationship and the object, diplomatically state the problem. After all, who wants to spend money on something that is never used?

BABY #3—Should you give another baby gift if you've already done so for babies one and two? Common sense is a good guide here. The point of a baby shower is to help the new mother feather her nest with clothes, stroller, and other paraphernalia. The hand-me-down machinery should then kick in for any successive brood.

THE GIFT OF MONEY—It may be tempting to ask for money instead of an object as a gift, but forswear the desire. Gifts should be freely given, not solicited. Be grateful for whatever someone has thought to give you.

EXCHANGING WITH A FRIEND OF MEANS—Clearly money wasn't the reason you two became friends, so don't let it become a matter of concern when exchanging gifts. You should spend only what you want, or are able to. This is not a contest.

RE-GIFTING—The quiet truth is that people do re-gift. Re-gifting is done with gifts that don't fit, aren't to your liking, or aren't returnable. Don't re-gift as a way of cleaning out your closet or saving money. As with any gift, the selection should be suited to the recipient.

MUSEUMS AND GALLERIES

NE TOUCHEZ PAS!—When you were a child, how many times did your mother tell you not to touch things in a store? The reprisal for such misbehavior in a museum or gallery is taken seriously, and is an inflexible rule worldwide. (Standing close to the art only works if you're not blocking anyone else's view.)

THE ART EXPERT—You know the type: he or she tends to recite at length (and loudly) on the artist, the brushstroke, the attention to detail, the quality of the print, or almost anything so as to convey Knowledge. But might doesn't equal right, so to all ad hoc experts and lecturers please don't pontificate on the paint. Lecture halls have seats; museums and galleries don't.

THE OUT-OF-TOWNERS—For many tourists, a visit almost anywhere isn't complete without the obligatory stop at the museum. Culture in any form is a blessing, so next time you find yourself looking at Egyptian hieroglyphs, enjoy the art, but please refrain from chatting about where you'll be having dinner. (Duane Hanson, where are you when we need you?)

MY CHILD COULD HAVE DRAWN THAT— This is a distinction only a privileged group can say, among them Picasso's mother, Matisse's father, de Kooning's parents.

IN A MUSEUM
SOLO VIEWING IS BLISS.

ANIMAL LOVERS

PET ALLERGIES—Being considerate of someone who's allergic to house pets is not simply a manners issue; often, it can be a serious concern for the person who has allergies. If you have pets, it's your obligation to let any first-time visitors know in advance. For some people, it's easy enough to take an allergy pill, but they will be less uncomfortable if you vacuum and dust before they arrive.

IT'S A CAT, NOT A KID—A painful point but true: Kenya, Gray Bear, Jasper, pretty-boy Frankie, and baby-cakes Sophie are not in the genus Homo sapiens. They're animals. So when you want to talk about your "children" around non-animal owners, have a heart and don't test their patience by talking at length about your little *snuggums*.

YOU LOVE DOGS, BUT...

When a friend's dog won't stop jumping on you and is not reprimanded by your friend, keep in mind that your response will be heard with biased ears. (The same thing applies to someone else's children.) Try to be friendly and make a joke, such as "This is the third dog today who's jumped on me. Dogs must love the color orange!" Dog owners everywhere, take note: the incorrigible pooch who yips, jumps, and sniffs is like a child in one basic way . . . in need of manners!

IN A MANNER OF SPEAKING...TO LET THE CAT OUT OF THE BAG

To disclose a secret. An old (and not very nice) country trick of substituting a cat for a pig in a burlap sack. If the buyer checked and saw that it was a cat, then the cat was let out of the bag. "People had long suspected that Charlie and his girlfriend might elope; just the same, the cat was let out of the bag when, unable to contain his enthusiasm, Charlie got into a discussion about diamond rings with his sister."

APARTMENT LIVING

IT'S MY PARTY—Everyone is entitled to give a party, and when you decide to have one, get in touch with those neighbors who might be inconvenienced. Sometimes it's nice to invite your neighbors as well, especially if you think they'll enjoy themselves. Weeknights are generally taboo for big or loud gatherings, and depending on where you live, the music should be lowered by 11:30 on the weekend. (No one, however, should have to tolerate a loud, tone-deaf drunk, night or day.)

GOOD KARMA IS A GOOD NEIGHBOR—Unless you have the luxury of a doorman, receiving packages can be an ordeal. If you will sign for a neighbor's package, hold open the elevator, or help walk a dog when it's owner is sick, this is the surest way for all of you to live harmoniously.

THAT'S NO CHILD, IT'S AN ELEPHANT—To a downstairs neighbor, children and high heels sound more like an invasion than a family happily at play. This is why carpets and rugs are the olive branch of high-rise dwellers. Be considerate and help to muffle ambient sound by covering your wood floors.

HAMMERS, FLOODS, AND THE TREADMILL

The idiosyncrasies of apartment living are as random as the people in any given building. There's the night owl who hangs pictures or vacuums at midnight, the absentminded tenant whose tub frequently runs over (and into your living room), and the sports nut whose *thump-thump-thump* at dawn gives you a major headache. Since what can't be tolerated must be changed, pick your battles wisely. Let reason, not bad temper, guide you. Protracted fighting among neighbors is a lose-lose situation.

THE GOOD SPORT

SNOW DAY—When it comes to skiing, nothing tops "safety first." If you're skiing with people less skilled, don't urge them to ski a more difficult slope. Slow down and go at their pace if you decide to join them at a level suited to their abilities. Pleasure and safety aren't mutually exclusive.

THE SUN WAS IN MY EYE—When kids don't turn in their homework, they pull out the proverbial "dog ate my homework" excuse. It never works. And in sports it never works to blame a poor shot on such things as the sun, worn-out tennis balls, someone else talking.

THAT'S MY BOBBY—Just because the little quarterback on the football field is your child, remember that every parent in the bleachers is rooting for their child, too. If you're annoyed when someone else is cheering and back-slapping about their son's victory, there's not much upside in saying something; instead, take a break and get yourself a hot dog. Clearly, one-upsmanship doesn't only occur on the playing field.

THREE GAMES TO LOVE—Kamikaze tennis is neither a civilized sport nor one to be played in mixed doubles. In competitive sports, tennis is one of the most elegant and gracious games, whether you're playing singles or doubles. It's natural to want to win, but win *well*—you and your opponent should be able to enjoy a post-match drink together.

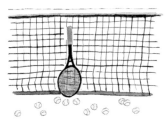

"I'D JUST AS SOON PLAY TENNIS
WITH THE NET DOWN."
—ROBERT FROST

TOUCHDOWN!—Victory does taste sweet, but don't let your enthusiasm become your opponent's poison. Learning to be a good sport applies to winning, too.

NO SPLASHING ALLOWED—A bully in the water is no less culpable than a bully on land. Don't splash others; only use a diving board for diving, not pushing; and never dunk or hold anyone under water. Water games are okay (remember "chicken"?), as long as you keep in mind that all of you are there to have *fun*.

KEEP YOUR COOL—The sky is blue, the weather is mild, even your golf shoes are darling, so why are you in a snit? For some players, golf is the ultimate in relaxation, akin to a pure zen moment. For others, though, that little golf ball comes to represent a metaphysical longing that remains relentlessly elusive. When sand traps and inner demons begin to handicap your game, slow down and gaze at the beauty around you. Nothing is more childish than a grown-up throwing a golf club on the green.

"ALWAYS IMITATE THE BEHAVIOR OF THE WINNERS WHEN YOU LOSE."

—GEORGE MEREDITH

IN A MANNER OF SPEAKING...RAIN CHECK

A ticket stub good for an event or performance deferred on account of rain; to make good on something at a later time. "Isaac had been looking forward to his first visit to the U.S. Open, but that morning it poured and the courts were too wet to play. His mother assured him they'd get a rain check, good for another day during the tournament."

MANNERS GO ABROAD
THANK YOU—MERCI—GRACIAS—DANKE SCHÖN

A generation or more ago, the proper lady and gentleman knew to follow custom in their dress and comportment wherever they traveled. Now, as Cole Porter wrote, "anything goes." Manners abroad, just like manners on your home turf, help life flow more smoothly and pleasantly. All you need are a few pointers.

COMPORTAMENTO EN PÚBLICO—OUT IN PUBLIC

One of the frequent salvos fired at Americans abroad is their overly casual style of dress. It needn't be so. The Louvre, for example, isn't a gymnasium, it's a museum. So leave your sneakers in your hotel room and don't wear sweat pants, either. On the subject of shoes, always remove them before entering a Japanese home or restaurant unless your host informs you otherwise. When you do so, be certain they're facing the door.

PARLA INGLESE?—No one abroad will expect you to speak their language fluently, but it is a sign of respect to learn how to speak some basic phrases. (The well-known exception is in France, especially Paris, where your perfect English is preferred to your broken French.)

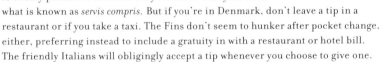

TIPPING—POURBOIRE—TRINKGELD

In many parts of Western Europe, a gratuity of ten to twenty percent is automatically included with your bill, what is known as *servis compris*. But if you're in Denmark, don't leave a tip in a restaurant or if you take a taxi. The Fins don't seem to hunker after pocket change, either, preferring instead to include a gratuity in with a restaurant or hotel bill. The friendly Italians will obligingly accept a tip whenever you choose to give one.

WHEN IT'S WISE TO DISCUSS A FEE IN ADVANCE OF SERVICES RENDERED— Next time you're in one of the Arab countries and wish to hire a car, especially one without a meter, confirm the fare with your driver before your journey. Protocol doesn't require you to tip, but if you want to be certain that your fare doesn't mysteriously double at the end of your ride, be sure to offer something.

TABLE MANNERS—VED BORDET

Don't go looking for a BLT sandwich when you're in France, or in Germany, or in Spain, or just about anywhere but in the United States. Culinary exploration and experimentation are what distinguish the gracious visitor from the small-minded tourist. Tapas in Spain, sushi in Japan, fresh herring in Denmark, or *cotoletta di tacchino alla bolognese* in Italy are what separate the rest of the world from the American melting pot. These distinctions are treasures to be savored. When you're in Japan, don't ask your waiter for a napkin—none are ever used. Instead, the Japanese carry around with them a small washcloth for such purposes.

REJSE—TRAVEL—VIAGGIO—VOYAGE

Every country has specific customs, which bear learning before you visit. In Austria, do bring flowers when invited to someone's home for dinner, but be sure they aren't red roses (unless you're feeling romantically inclined). The Germans will heartily shake your hand upon arriving and leaving, the British may proffer you a rather weak one, and the Greeks may embrace you. As for the British, it's considered indiscreet to inquire after someone's profession when first meeting. The French find any direct inquiry potentially inflammatory, so it's best to follow the lead of your host. In Japan, the women send chocolates to men on Valentine's Day; a month later, the favor is returned.

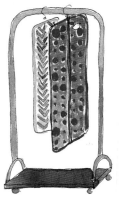

Punctuality is a many varied thing from country to country. Americans straddle the middle road compared to their foreign counterparts, which suggests, like everything else involved with international travel, that when in Rome do as the Romans do.

MONEY MATTERS

NEGOTIATING—There's a reason why some companies hire professional negotiators to mediate contracts; like many things in life, negotiating is an art. Or at the very least, a talent, which some people naturally have. Feel free to haggle at an open-air flea market where chairs and old record albums and silver coasters can be found. You might even be able to shave a few dollars off something at an antique shop where you have a prior relationship with the proprietor. Where should you pay the sticker price without quibble or dissent?—At a vintage clothing shop, farmer's market, your beauty salon.

INAPPROPRIATE CHARGE—Math may be perfect, but for those of us who do the adding and subtracting, there is always room for error. Always check an itemized bill, be it at the grocery store, restaurant, or hotel. If you find you've been overcharged (or undercharged, for which you deserve an A+ for honesty), quietly speak to the person responsible for your bill. Like so many mistakes, this one was unintentional.

WHEN THE BILL COMES—While everyone else was eating shrimp cocktail and hangar steak, you were nibbling on greens with goat cheese. Then the bill comes and your share is $48. Ouch. For those awkward times when you've eaten considerably less than others with whom you're splitting the bill, be prepared to pay up. When it comes to money, "fair" doesn't always come into play.

STICKER SHOCK—You're at the flower shop, and the New Zealand peonies you covet cost $6. Or so you thought until you got to the counter and learned that they are $6 *a stem*. Be honest and make a simple apology (don't go overboard). Settle on snapdragons instead.

DID YOU PAY RETAIL?

There can be a fine line between interest and envy. Before you ask a friend the price of her new dress, ask yourself why you want to know. Frankly, most people are uncomfortable talking about what they paid for something, and among women the subject may make them a wee testy.

"NEITHER A BORROWER NOR A LENDER BE."

—SHAKESPEARE

ANDY'S TRUISMS

It's difficult to look elegant while eating a chili dog.

Making others feel good makes you feel good.

When you insult another, you insult yourself.

Garlic, onions, and kisses simply don't mix.

Wearing a lobster bib doesn't strip a man of his masculinity.

Being kind doesn't equal being meek.

Sleep with the enemy and wake up without friends.

EXCEPTIONS TO EVERY RULE

You may start eating before everyone else if you have
hypoglycemia or another medical condition (besides rudeness.)

You should pay the check if you invited the couple to
dinner as your guests. However, if they slip their credit
card to the waiter first or threaten you with a steak
knife and insist on paying, then let it go.

Patience is a virtue, unless someone is taking advantage of you.

Be alert. We need more lerts.

THANK YOU

It seems that every project I venture upon involves the helping hands of many people, and this book is no exception. Everyone has pitched in—from my husband and colleagues at *kate spade* to my dog, Henry, who earnestly practices good manners everyday.

Julia Leach, who oversees our creative department and is a longtime friend of Andy's and mine, has truly shouldered the responsibility of putting this book together. I don't know how she manages to have so much energy and such grace under pressure, but she is a god-send. Working in tandem with Julia is our editor and new friend, Ruth Peltason, whose enthusiasm and expertise has helped all of us make this book special. They were joined in their efforts by Virginia Johnson, our gifted illustrator; designer Alberta Testanero, who gave the book its overall look; and Ana Rogers, who took the vision for this book and brought it to life.

Our business partners, Elyce Arons and Pamela Bell, and I were friends long before we started this company, and they have been greatly supportive of this project. Their suggestions, their own experiences, and those we've shared have all contributed to *Manners*. So has the friendship and encouragement extended by Robin Marino, president of *kate spade*. I'm also grateful to Marybeth Schmitt, who has skillfully navigated our publicity efforts. Also at our office I would like to thank Susan Anthony, Barbara Kolsun, Stacy Van Praagh, Meg Touborg, and everyone in our creative department—Biz Zast , Lawren Howell, Jenifer Ruske, Cheree Berry, Naseem Niaraki, and Anthony Coombs. Christine Muhlke, who provided the research, was also invaluable for her natural smarts and good ideas.

For years I've looked to Emily Post for guidance and wisdom. Of the many women who have been challenged by the task of guiding Americans along the course of good manners, Emily Post has done so with charm, grace, and good humor. Her advice on so many subjects remains the best advice to be found, and even though *Etiquette* was published more than eighty years ago, Emily Post still sounds natural and unaffected. She's my idea of a national treasure.

The business of publishing a book is new to me, and I am grateful that our agent, Ira Silverberg, has been so wonderfully wise. I have been fortunate to work with the devoted crew at Simon & Schuster, including David Rosenthal, executive vice president and publisher, whose enthusiasm wowed us all; Amanda Murray, our patient in-house editor; Walter L. Weintz; Michael Selleck; Tracey Guest; Peter McCulloch; and Sybil Pincus. Thank you, thank you.

And then there's my husband, Andy, who first gave me the courage to go into business more than a decade ago and now into books. "We already have so many books and we both love to read," I told him, "do you really think it's a good idea to try being an author?" Well, his answer is before you. Humor and kindness are high on my list of important qualities in a person, and I'm fortunate to have found in Andy a rare combination of both. His ideas and his infectious spirit and voice are in *Manners*, page for page. So, too, is Andy's encouragement, his humor, and his love. I am indeed blessed.

Kate Spade

SELECT
BIBLIOGRAPHY

Axtell, Richard, ed. *Do's and Taboos Around the World*. Comp., The Parker Pen Company. New York: John Wiley & Sons, Inc. 1993.

Baldridge, Letitia. *Letitia Baldridge's Complete Guide to the New Manners for the '90s*. New York: Rawson Associates (div. of Macmillan Publishing), 1990.

Barr, Norah K., Marsha Moran, and Patrick Moran, comp. *M.F.K. Fisher: A Life in Letters*. Washington, D.C.: Counterpoint, 1998.

Benton, Frances, with the General Foundation of Women's Clubs. *Etiquette: The Complete Modern Guide for Day-to-Day Living the Correct Way*. New York: Random House, 1956.

Esar, Evan. *20,000 Quips & Quotes: A Treasury of Witty Remarks, Comic Proverbs, Wisecracks, and Epigrams*. New York: Barnes & Noble Books, 1995.

Feinberg, Steven L. *Crane's Blue Book of Stationery*. Foreword by Stanley Marcus. New York: Doubleday, 1989.

Martin, Judith. *Miss Manners' Guide to Excruciatingly Correct Behavior*. New York: Galahad Books, 1982.

Moats, Alice-Leone. *No Nice Girl Swears*. Foreword by Edna Woolman Chase. New York: Blue Ribbon Books, Inc., 1934.

Morris, William and Mary Morris. *Morris Dictionary of Words and Phrase Origins*. 2nd ed. Foreword by Isaac Asimov. New York: HarperCollins Publishers, 1988.

Osgood, Charles. *Funny Letters from Famous People*. New York: Broadway Books, 2003.

Post, Emily. *Etiquette: The Blue Book of Social Usage*. New York: Funk & Wagnalls Co., Publishers, 1945. Reprint 1949.

Post, Peter. *Essential Manners for Men: What to Do, When to Do It, and Why*. New York: HarperResource, 2003.

Rosenkrantz, Linda. *Telegram!* New York: Henry Holt and Company, 2003.

Soames, Mary, ed. *Winston and Clementine: The Personal Letters of the Churchills*. Boston: Mariner Books, 2001.

Tiffany's Table Manners for Teenagers. Introduction by Walter Hoving. Illustrations by Joe Eula. New York: Ives Washburn, Inc., 1961.

Tiger, Caroline. *How to Behave: A Guide to Modern Manners for the Socially Challenged*. Philadelphia: Quirk Books, 2003.

THE POLITE TRAVELER GOES ABROAD
FRENCH
I'd like to check my raincoat and small dog, Edna.

J'aimerais laisser mon imperméable et ma petite chienne Edna au vestiaire.

NORWEGIAN
Pardon me, sir, could you please help me open my Lime Rickey?

Unskyld meg, min herre, kan de vaere så snill å hjelpe meg åpne min "lime rickey"?

ITALIAN
I need to thank our hostess for taking us to the opera, even though it was six hours long.

Devo ringraziare il nostro ospite per averci portato all' opera, anche se e' durata per sei ore.

PORTUGUESE
Operator, could you please connect me to BUtterfield-8?

Telefonista, por favor me transfira para a "BUtterfield-8?"

Editors: Ruth A. Peltason, for Bespoke Books
           Julia Leach, for kate spade

Designers: Ana Rogers
           Alberta Testanero, for kate spade

The author and publisher gratefully acknowledge those writers whose works contributed to this book.

"This Is Just to Say" by William Carlos Williams, from *Collected Poems: 1909–1939, Volume 1,* copyright © 1938 by New Directions Publishing Corp. Reprinted by permission of New Directions Publishing Corp.

SIMON & SCHUSTER
Rockefeller Center
1230 Avenue of the Americas
New York, NY 10020

For information regarding special discounts for bulk purchases, please contact
Simon & Schuster Special Sales at 1-800-456-6798 or business@simonandschuster.com

Manufactured in Italy

10 9 8 7 6 5 4 3 2 1

Library of Congress Cataloging-in-Publication Data

Spade, Kate.
   Manners : always gracious, sometimes irreverent / by Kate Spade ; edited by Ruth
Peltason and Julia Leach ; illustrations by Virginia Johnson.
      p. cm.
   Includes bibliographical references.
   1. Etiquette. I. Peltason, Ruth A. II. Leach, Julia (Julia E.) III. Title.

BJ1853.S67 2004
395–dc22

2003062970

ISBN 0-7432-5066-4